Florida's Fossils

Florida's Fossils

Guide to Location, Identification and Enjoyment

Revised Edition

Robin C. Brown

Pineapple Press
Sarasota, Florida

This book is dedicated to my wife, Jan, with my love and thanks

Inquiries should be addressed to:

Pineapple Press, Inc.
P.O. Box 3889
Sarasota, Florida 34230

www.pineapplepress.com

ISBN: 978-1-56164-571-8 (pb)

The Library of Congress has catalogued the hardback as follows:

Brown, Robin C., 1934–
    Florida's fossils: guide to location, identification, and enjoyment / Robin C. Brown—3rd ed.
                    p.   cm.
Includes index.
ISBN 978-1-56164-409-4 (alk. paper)
1. Fossils–Florida. I. Title.

QE747.F6B76   2008
560'.9759—dc22

                                                        2007048013

Third Edition
10 9 8 7 6 5 4 3 2 1

Design by Frank Cochrane Associates, Sarasota, Florida
Composition by Lubin Typesetting and Literary Services, Sarasota, Florida
Printed in the United States of America

Author's Note

This book is my thanks to Florida, a state with a unique record of past life. The search for Florida's fossils has taken me to some of the most exciting and beautiful places imaginable and has afforded the opportunity to work with wonderful people. I am sincerely grateful.

Often, though, my fossil finds posed a multitude of questions that appeared unanswerable. General books about fossils rarely helped me to understand Florida's fossils; the orderly layers of land and sea creatures the books described just weren't to be found. What I saw was a glorious jumble of fossilized fish, land snails, horse teeth, alligators, sea shells, and tortoises. Over and over I wondered, "How in the world did this come to be?"

Many answers were there, when the right person or publication was finally found. This book is aimed at providing that information in language understandable to the beginning fossil hunter. It is the result of 25 years' interest in Florida's fossils. There is no way to list all who have encouraged, inspired, and contributed to its writing, but special thanks are due the following people:

To F. Stearns MacNeil and Durward Boggess, of the U.S. Geological Survey, who answered some of my earliest questions.

To Michael Hansinger, who introduced me to the Florida Museum of Natural History and who generously helped with all aspects of this book.

To S. David Webb and Bruce MacFadden, who offered information, encouragement, and editorial advice, and made the vertebrate paleontology resources of the Florida Museum of Natural History available to me.

To Douglas Jones, who furnished insights into the ancient sea out of which Florida rose, and the invertebrates that populated it.

To Gary Morgan and Roger Portell, whose knowledge of the Florida Museum of Natural History's paleontology collections made it possible for me to study, measure, and photograph hundreds of specimens.

To the late Howard Converse and to Russ McCarty, who provided information about fossil preparation and preservation.

To Ann Pratt and Richard Hulbert, who helped with every part of the book from scope and format to choice of photographs.

To the many collectors around the state who told me of places where fossils could be found, techniques for finding them, and adventures encountered in the hunt. Of these, particular thanks to Frank Garcia, James Haisten, Cliff Jeremiah, Lewis Ober, Don Serbosek, Ben Waller, and

The author with his son, Stephen Brown. Photograph by Stuart Brown.

5

Wayne Wooten. And to Joe Latvis, who expressed so well the point of view of the amateur fossil hunter and who taught me the joys of river diving.

To Anita and Ed Brown, who introduced me to the Florida Paleontological Society and who have done so much to further the excellence of that organization.

To Miriam and Howard Schriner, whose outstanding work in the Caloosahatchee Formation of southwest Florida furnishes a superb example of what the educated amateur can accomplish.

To Frank Rupert at the Florida Bureau of Geology, who gave such excellent help with ancient shorelines.

To Chris Kreider and Eleanor Mobley, who did original paintings and drawings for the book.

To Kay and Sandy Young, who opened their hearts and home to my entire family during the writing of this book and shared with us the thrill of the hunt.

To my four children, Deirdre, Cotten, Stuart, and Stephen, who have hunted fossils with me all their lives. They have supported this effort with everything from scholarly critique to brute force.

And finally, to my wife Jan, whose loving encouragement and skillful editing made the book possible, but who stubbornly refuses to be acknowledged as its co-author.

CONTENTS

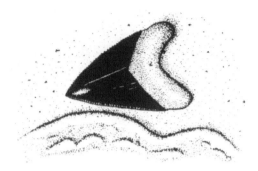

PROLOGUE

In the early morning stillness, the eastern horizon lightens over the wide sands of Melbourne Beach. Inland from the expensive high-rise condominiums fringing the Atlantic shore, back across Indian River Sound where the land is cheaper, a conical pile of white limerock towers above the edge of a quarry. The warm light of the just-risen sun picks out a scatter of fossil horse teeth spilling down its slope. These are teeth of an animal that evolved on this continent over a period of sixty million years, mysteriously vanished, then, after an absence of ten thousand years, returned with European explorers.

In the center of the Florida peninsula, morning light creeps down a steep bank of the Withlacoochee River. For weeks the swirling water has been undercutting the sands of this river bend. With a sigh, a twenty-foot stretch of bank slides into the stream. The foaming river smooths and spreads the sand. From the surface of this newly formed beach gleams a ribbed tooth as big as a man's head. Its polished grinding surface once crushed vegetation for an enormous elephant, the Columbian Mammoth.

The sun climbs higher in the east, warming the air in the Everglades. It also warms masses of limestone along an arrow-straight canal which separates sawgrass marsh from clumps of cypress. Between the flat limestone rocks are pockets of white sand — miniature remnants of an ancient beach. Here and there, protruding from the sand, are perfect disks, each bearing a delicately looped star pattern. These are extinct sand dollars, leftovers of the shallow sea that was Florida five million years ago.

As noon approaches, the sunlight reaches down into the clear waters of the Ichetucknee River. Ripples on the surface make a moving pattern on gravel ten feet below.

Tape grass undulates in the strong current. A black object, silvered with bubbles, tumbles along in the swift stream. It settles into the quiet of a small hollow and trails slow spirals of mud. An hour later, cleaned by the flowing water, the object is identifiable as a skull with huge canine teeth — all that remains of an enormous saber-toothed cat that preyed on the countless animals of Florida's plains twelve thousand years ago.

Inland from the blackrush marshes of the upper Gulf coast, cumulus clouds thicken in the afternoon heat. Sunlight comes and goes through the branches of huge hardwoods on the banks of the Steinhatchee River. The dark water is low, exposing pitted limestone sills, slick with moss. In a rock pool, a row of white pyramids glints in the shifting light — the upper jaw and teeth of a large tapir whose descendents today are found only in Malaysia and South America.

In South Florida, the afternoon thunderstorms are about to begin. Black clouds build over piles of sand and rock in a shell pit near the town of LaBelle. A cool wind suddenly sweeps from the cloud mass and torrential rain begins to fall, sending white rivulets down the sides of the tall piles. The shells are washed clean. The storm ends as suddenly as it began and the westering sun lights a sparkling cascade of snow-white shapes. Massive conchs, unknown to any modern beach, lie amid a profusion of top shells, bubble shells, and tiny marginellas. Scattered here and there are lacy murexes with extravagant fronds and whorls. A perfect cowrie glows with the same sheen that it exhibited on an ancient beach. These are shells of the three-million-year-old Caloosahatchee Formation, prized by collectors the world over.

Now the sun is low; it hangs just above the waters of the Gulf of Mexico. The storm remains only as a few clouds glowing on the western horizon. Low-energy waves lap the smooth sands of Casey Key. As a wave recedes, a patch of foam slowly disperses, revealing a gleaming saw-edged triangle three inches long. It is a tooth of the largest carnivorous shark that ever lived: *Carcharodon megalodon*, gone from the world's seas for a million years.

The sun disappears below the horizon. Night falls.

Fossils are abundant in Florida's streams and rivers.

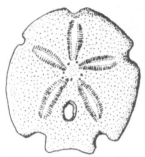

Encope tamiamiensis

CHAPTER 1

Florida: A Great Place to Find Fossils

Giant ground sloth.

Saber-tooth cat.

Mastodon.

Florida's 50-million-year fossil history contains some of the most fascinating land and sea animals that ever lived: exotic sharks and whales, huge mammoths and mastodons, fierce cats with nine-inch saber teeth, vampire bats, and improbable giant sloths that could reach 20 feet into treetops to browse on tender leaves.

Searching for the remains of these ancient creatures is real adventure, whether it's done by walking along a quiet stream bank or exploring the bottom of the Gulf of Mexico with SCUBA.

And the fossil finds are often real trophies. Few natural objects rival the gleaming beauty of an Ice Age mastodon tooth; no modern shell excels the lacy elegance of a three-million-year-old murex.

Evidence of past life is amazingly abundant in Florida. Many areas of North America have no fossils at all. In areas where fossils do occur, the specimens usually consist of mollusks, corals, or crinoids — animals without backbones called invertebrates. In rare places where vertebrate animal remains can be found, the fossils are usually encased in rocks that are hard to reach and tedious to dig out. And seldom are such finds in good condition. But in Florida, fossils are different. Even the usual definition of fossil, "any trace of ancient life found in the rocks," doesn't fit very well.

Few Florida fossils are in rock. They are more likely to be found lying loose in beach sand or river gravel. In fact, fossils turn up everywhere. Florida roads are built on foundations made of fossil sea creatures. The bones of extinct animals are constantly being exposed on river banks and roadcuts. Most loads of fill dirt and limerock are laden with fossil shells, sea urchins, and corals. Everywhere, ancient animal remains lie close to the surface waiting to be discovered.

For many fossil hunters, bones of extinct vertebrates — animals with backbones whose skeletons are similar to our own — are the most exciting finds. Vertebrate fossils are surprisingly plentiful in Florida. The remains of most vertebrates occur as scattered bones or teeth, and some locations contain vast numbers of them. Occasionally, the parts of an entire beast will turn up.

There were no dinosaurs in Florida (dinosaurs became extinct 65 million years ago), but the 50-million-year record that does exist covers the last three-fourths of the Age of Mammals, a time when animal life was wonderfully abundant. The hunt is even more exciting because experts say the variety of fossil creatures found to date is probably less than half of that still undiscovered! Each year, species previously unknown in Florida are found — often by amateur fossil hunters.

The three-million-year-old murex *Chicoreus brevifrons*.

Twelve-million-year-old shells from a creek in Florida's panhandle.

An ancient sea urchin encased in Eocene limestone before and after removal.

About 25 million years ago Florida began to emerge from the sea. But this emergence was not an uninterrupted process. The sea rose and partially reclaimed the land on many occasions and once or twice nearly got it all. These immersions and erosions produced some interesting scrambling of the fossil record. Sea creatures, bay and estuary dwellers, fresh water animals, and land beasts are often jumbled together in complex profusion. Generalizations about what kind of fossil is found where are hard to make.

Very generally, the oldest land animals are found in higher elevations in the northern third of the state and along the central ridge. But the wonderful creatures of Florida's last two million years, the Pleistocene animals, are mixed in everywhere: overlying older beds, on river bottoms, in limestone fissures, buried in ancient swamps and lakes . . . everywhere.

An overview of the state's fossil distribution shows the following:

In the panhandle, rivers from the Chipola to the Steinhatchee are good sources of Pleistocene animal remains. And not only the large rivers have fossils. Streams, springs, and spring runs all contain bones and teeth of extinct creatures such as saber-tooth cat, mammoth, and dire wolf. Along a creek in Calhoun County are beautiful 12-million-year-old seashells.

On the East Coast, Atlantic breakers wash up fossil land animals on Jacksonville Beach — bones and teeth of bison, horse, and giant ground sloths that once roamed a coastal plain when glaciers covered much of North America.

The central ridge of Florida is made up of ancient marine limestone. Because limestone is easily dissolved by surface waters, the state's "backbone" is riddled like a huge sponge with interconnecting holes. From time to time during Florida's past, holes opened to the surface and captured the animals then living. Some holes first became caves and were a home to bats, whose bones layered the cave floor. When the roof of the cave collapsed to form a deep pit, surface animals fell in and their bones contributed a new layer. Many of the holes eventually became ponds that added fish, turtles, and frogs to the bone pile. In North-Central Florida, these fossil treasure troves are sometimes uncovered by quarries or rivers. Some remain as mysteriously beautiful pools, far from any river or stream.

Halfway down the peninsula, phosphate mining uncovers ancient shorelines 2 to 15 million years old that at different times were home to both land and sea creatures. Gigantic dragline buckets bring up bones of

A sinkhole in Jefferson County.

Shark tooth on Venice beach.

camel and mastodon mixed with whale vertebrae and the ribs of sea cows.

South of Tampa, a river system that no longer exists once carried quantities of bones to a nameless bay. As a result, fossils of land animals that lived a million years ago now surface along what today is called Apollo Beach.

Along the lower Gulf coast, Venice Beach receives a bounty of shark teeth, endlessly renewed from an offshore marine deposit.

Inland, in South Florida, rock mining operations turn fossil shells into roadbed material. Wonderful varieties of sea bottom creatures are brought to light by these operations. Beautifully preserved shells, barnacles, and corals ranging in age from one to four million years are piled in profusion around quarry pits.

This book tells how to look for Florida's fossils and how to identify these ancient animals. For those who would like to know more about the past, it traces Florida's prehistory and the remarkable creatures that were part of it. And most important, it gives proven sites around the state where fossil hunters make exciting finds year after year.

On sandy beaches, along tree-lined rivers, or in crystal clear springs, the hunt is always challenging. The fossils are constantly changing. Every tide, every rain, every swirl of rushing water reveals new treasures. Discovery awaits!

Fossil shells and coral from Hendry County. (Photograph by Stuart Brown)

Shark teeth are so abundant at Venice Beach that sporting goods stores stock special scoops for the fossil enthusiast.

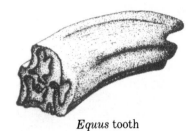

Equus tooth

CHAPTER 2

How and Where to Look

Fossils from the Peace River — eight different fossil animals should be identifiable in this pile.

The first part of this chapter describes the general areas likely to yield fossils. Specific sites and the types of fossils found in each site are listed in the second part.

How to Spot Fossils

Anywhere in Florida that the land is weathered, washed, eroded, leveled, mined, drained, or disturbed in any way, fossils are likely to turn up.

When searching, several clues help to pick out fossils from surrounding sand, rocks, or fragmented shells. The **color** of bone and teeth is often dark — brown, black, gray, or blue-gray — and contrasts with the lighter background material. This is particularly striking in shell and limestone layers where the predominant color is white. **Texture** can be a good fossil indicator. Teeth have smooth, shiny enamel. Bone is smooth on the outside (cortical bone) and sponge-like inside (cancellous bone). The bony plates beneath the skin of alligators and the shells of certain turtles have a characteristic pitted surface. **Shape** is important in spotting fossils. The teeth of many grass-eaters have distinctive parallel ridges and complex patterns of folded enamel. The triangular shape and serrated edges of shark teeth quickly become familiar.

Screenwashing fossils in a South Florida creek.

Rivers and Streams

Florida's streams and rivers are beautiful places. Almost any of them that are accessible and have a good flow are likely to be a source of fossils. Hunting is best and water is clearest at times of low water level: summer and fall in North Florida, and winter and spring in Central and South Florida.

Walk along river banks and examine vertically cut banks for fossils in their original undisturbed position (*in situ*). The relationship of a fossil to surrounding fossils or other earth layers gives information about its age and how it became fossilized. This is explained in chapters six and eight.

Search the stream edge. At times of low water, fossils are often uncovered.

Wade in shallow water (wearing old tennis shoes is a good idea) and look for gravel-covered bottom areas. Stretches of gravel may occur anywhere, but they tend to form just downstream from rapids. Screenwashing the gravel in a shallow box having a bottom made of 1/4 inch mesh hardware cloth (see Chapter 4 on equipment) will likely yield shark teeth and sometimes the bones and teeth of land animals.

Explore with a mask. A bottom mixture of sand and gravel can be separated by "fanning" with hands or feet.

Recovery of whale vertebra from a stream in Lee County.

Although any gravel is likely to yield fossils, coarser gravel is more easily screened and the fossils are more readily seen. On shallow rocky bottoms, look for pits in rocks which often contain gravel fossils.

If you are a good swimmer, use snorkel and fins to search deeper places at river bends. Large bones and teeth often settle here.

When working the bottom of a swiftly flowing stream, tie a rope to an upstream tree and let it trail downstream. Hold onto it to maintain position while hunting under water. If you are qualified in SCUBA diving, bottom exploration can be done by letting the river current carry you downstream while hunting. Deep holes can be more thoroughly investigated with SCUBA.

A canoe or kayak provides means for much more exploration. Most of Florida's fossil-rich rivers have canoe rental facilities located along them. On the Web, search "canoe rentals Florida." If you have your own canoe, put in at a public ramp or highway crossing. If the current isn't too swift, paddle *upstream* marking good spots, then drift back downstream and explore each spot more thoroughly. If the water is clear, use mask and snorkel and float beside the canoe. Inspect the bottom as the current, it's a good idea to plan a *downstream* float trip. Park a car at the downstream take-out spot and, with a second car, take the canoe to the upstream put-in point to begin your trip. A downstream trip is easier, but explore each likely fossil spot as you come to it. After you've passed, paddling back to find it again will be hard work!

Quarries

In Florida, most quarries are excavations for limerock. The rock is usually made up of creatures that lived in the ancient seas. Some limestones have compacted over millions of years; some remain a loose mix of individual specimens. The fossils available in these limestones are largely marine invertebrates: shells, sand dollars, barnacles, and corals. Mixed in are occasional shark teeth, parts of bony fish, and bones of marine mammals such as sea cow, dolphin, and whale. Depending on location, the age of the limestone may be from a few thousand to 50 million years.

Sometimes in the upper layers or in the overburden (sand or clay removed to expose the limerock), pockets or fossilized land animals (terrestrial vertebrates) can be found.

The vertical faces found in quarries are excellent places to study fossil layers. Fossils are often washed out of these banks and collect along the base. Some operations crush limerock for roadbed and other construction; few fossils survive this treatment. But piles of uncrushed

A quarry in Lafayette County.

Mold of Eocene mollusk *Architectonica* from Sumter County.

material are good hunting sites, particularly after a rain.

The quarries of North and North-Central Florida expose limestones which are soft, very white, and composed of almost pure calcium carbonate. They contain the impressions or molds of many fossil mollusks (shells). The two principal limestone units are the Ocala and the Suwannee.

Ocala Limestone was formed in the Eocene epoch, about 40 million years ago (the geologic time table on page 33 shows the five epochs important to Florida prehistory) and contains upwards of 30 species of beautifully preserved sea urchins and sand dollars (echinoids). In some areas there are numerous coin-shaped outer casings of single-celled marine animals, called foraminifera, embedded in the limestone. Fossil crabs and shark teeth occasionally turn up in the Ocala Limestone.

Suwannee Limestone is about 30 million years old. In addition to mollusks, it contains some echinoids, notably the sea urchin *Rhyncholampas gouldi.*

Both the Suwannee and Ocala limestones are exposed in rock quarries from Jefferson to Pasco counties and in the panhandle in Jackson County. Suwannee Limestone is exposed along the banks of the Suwannee River in Columbia County. (See the map of Florida geologic formations on page 32.)

Along the central and southern Gulf coast, quarrying exposes several remarkable assemblages of mollusks. Beginning with the oldest, these are the Tamiami, Caloosahatchee, and Fort Thompson formations.

In the Tamiami Formation, the shells, barnacles, and corals were living members of a sea bottom 3 to 5 million years ago (late Miocene to early Pliocene). In Lee, Hendry, and Collier counties, little remains of the Tamiami mollusks except internal and external molds, the impressions of the inside and outside of their shells. But at quarries in Sarasota and Charlotte counties and along the Kissimmee River, beautiful shells of the Pinecrest Member of the Tamiami Formation are found. Among these are giant barnacles, pectens, and a sand dollar called *Encope tamiamiensis.*

The Caloosahatchee Formation represents a sea bottom of Pliocene-Pleistocene age and it is wonderfully preserved. Mixed with an enormous variety of mollusks are branching corals, coral heads, barnacles, sea urchins, and parts of crabs. These creatures lived one to three million years ago and 50 percent of the species represented are now extinct.

The Fort Thompson Formation is Pleistocene in age, deposited during portions of the last million years, and

Foraminifera or "coin fossils" in Ocala Limestone, Lafayette County — Overall size 4¾ x 2¾ inches (12 x 7 cm).

consists of collections of sea life similar to those found on beaches and shallow bays today. The state of preservation is good and the fossil assemblage looks a lot like a modern beach. The Fort Thompson Formation overlies the Caloosahatchee Formation in many areas.

Phosphate Mines

Florida's phosphate pits are gigantic strip mining operations. Ore is excavated by huge draglines with buckets the size of a two-car garage. Mines are available for fossiling only by organized tour. The Florida Paleontological Society and local fossil clubs often set up field trips to these sites.

Phosphate mining is a major industry in Florida. Mines are located in Polk, Hillsborough, Hardee, Manatee, and De Soto counties, and the huge pits expose Miocene-Pliocene age fauna (animals) from the Bone Valley Formation. Known the world over, Bone Valley fossils are a mixture of marine (sea), estuarine (brackish water), freshwater, and terrestrial (land) vertebrates. Shark and manatee are found adjacent to rhinoceros, horse, and extinct pond turtle. These complex deposits originated in bays, rivers, and coastal plains, beginning about 15 million years ago in the Miocene and ending about three million years ago in the Pliocene. (See the chart of Florida's geologic epochs on page 33.) In the upper layers or overburden — sand and muck moved to expose the phosphate — are found Pleistocene animals from two million to ten thousand years old.

Filled Areas

Much of the land development in Florida is done by digging out low-lying marsh areas to make lakes, then using the acquired fill dirt to raise the level of the surrounding land. Since marsh terrain is often an excellent place to find Pleistocene vertebrate fossils, the muck and swamp bottom that has been dug up and spread over the land produces a good area for hunting. The best finds on filled areas are made after rains and before the vegetation begins to grow.

Sinkholes

Sinkholes are interesting geologic features of North and Central Florida. A sinkhole usually begins as a vertical fissure or a solution hole in limestone. In time it may also expand horizontally along the water table, thus becoming a submerged cave. When the ground water level drops and the cave becomes air-filled, the unsupported roof may collapse, producing an excellent animal trap. Sinkholes "sampled" vertebrates at inter-

Fort Thompson Formation shells in a Hendry County quarry.

vals throughout Florida's history, providing wonderfully preserved arrays of animals living when the sink was open — time capsules of local life.

Filled sinkholes that have accidentally been uncovered represent some of the most important fossil sites in Florida. Sinkholes trapped animals during every age of Florida's fossil past. The most famous is the Thomas Farm bone bed in Gilchrist County, an 18-million-year-old early Miocene sinkhole site that has been worked by paleontologists since 1932. Thomas Farm is usually available only to professionals, but field trips for amateurs are occasionally arranged by the Florida Museum of Natural History.

When a river or stream cuts through a sinkhole deposit, spectacular fossil finds result. Large bones are often clustered in a limited area along the river bottom; small bones may be washed downstream for considerable distances. Some sinkholes are open and still trapping animals. In these, bones may date from last week back to a million years ago.

Many sinkholes are partially filled with water. Fossil hunting in such sites is exceedingly dangerous. Only teams trained in cave diving should attempt it.

Canals

In the construction of canals, draglines sometimes bring up fossil bones and teeth, often little damaged by their trip in the dragline bucket. Occasionally the fossil material can be traced to its original site in the canal bank. Remember, the deepest material generally winds up on the *top* of the spoil pile beside the canal.

In canal hunting, a lot of walking is usually necessary. Canals cut through many terrains. Marine fossils such as shells and corals may be exposed along much of the cut, but terrestrial vertebrates are usually in pockets. Persistence is needed when hunting canals. The best time to hunt is when the excavation is a few weeks old and just after a rain.

Beaches

On some Florida beaches, fossils can be found in great abundance. Offshore fossil deposits are eroded by currents and wave action, and bones and teeth wash ashore. Many West Coast beaches — especially from Casey Key (south of Sarasota) to Manasota Key (Englewood) yield enormous numbers of Miocene and Pliocene shark teeth and occasional Pleistocene vertebrate remains. Similar but less abundant material washes up on the East Coast from Fernandina Beach down to Vero Beach. In Tampa Bay, early Pleistocene fossils are found at Apollo Beach.

Look along the water's edge and screen the shelly layer where waves are breaking. Larger bones and teeth wash in after a storm.

SCUBA makes it possible to recover offshore fossil material before it is subjected to wave action. Good bottom hunting sites are found off Venice Beach only a few hundred feet from shore.

How to Find Good Fossil Localities In Your Area

1. Join a fossil club. There are several regional clubs in Florida. Members can tell you good places to hunt. Group field trips can often hunt areas not open to individuals.
2. Join the Florida Paleontological Society, the statewide organization for amateur fossil hunters. Meetings are held twice a year. To join, write:

    Florida Paleontological Society, Inc.
    Florida Museum of Natural History
    University of Florida
    Gainesville, FL 32611
3. Ask the staff of the local nature center or natural history museum about good fossil exposures near

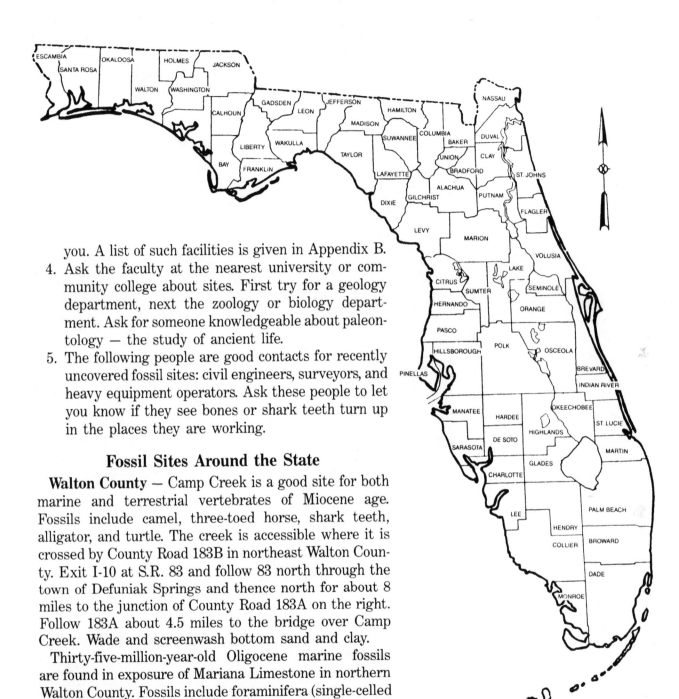

Map of Florida Counties.

you. A list of such facilities is given in Appendix B.
4. Ask the faculty at the nearest university or community college about sites. First try for a geology department, next the zoology or biology department. Ask for someone knowledgeable about paleontology — the study of ancient life.
5. The following people are good contacts for recently uncovered fossil sites: civil engineers, surveyors, and heavy equipment operators. Ask these people to let you know if they see bones or shark teeth turn up in the places they are working.

Fossil Sites Around the State

Walton County — Camp Creek is a good site for both marine and terrestrial vertebrates of Miocene age. Fossils include camel, three-toed horse, shark teeth, alligator, and turtle. The creek is accessible where it is crossed by County Road 183B in northeast Walton County. Exit I-10 at S.R. 83 and follow 83 north through the town of Defuniak Springs and thence north for about 8 miles to the junction of County Road 183A on the right. Follow 183A about 4.5 miles to the bridge over Camp Creek. Wade and screenwash bottom sand and clay.

Thirty-five-million-year-old Oligocene marine fossils are found in exposure of Mariana Limestone in northern Walton County. Fossils include foraminifera (single-celled marine animals), molds of mollusks and corals, and marine vertebrates such as fish bones and ray mouth plates and barbs. Near the Alabama-Florida line, about four miles west of Gaskin, is Natural Bridge. Continue on 183A northeast for about one mile and turn left on 183B. Take 183B northwest to return to S.R. 83 at Glendale. Go north on 83 about 8 miles to County Road 181. Go left on 181 about 5 miles to a unpaved road on the left. This road crosses a natural bridge hollowed out by the

Geologic Formations

Youngest Rocks

Series	Symbol	Formation & Member	Description
Recent and Pleistocene	Qmt	Several lower marine and estuarine deposits	Fresh water marls, peats, sands, muds, now forming in stream valleys and freshwater lakes and marine sediments accumulating along shorelines and shelves of the Gulf of Mexico and the Atlantic Ocean
	Qtm	Lake Flirt Marl occurs in Lake Flirt area, Glades County (not shown at this scale)	
Pleistocene	Qa	Anastasia Formation	In South Florida the Pleistocene is represented by limestone, shell hash, clay and sand
	Qmo	Miami Oolite	
	Qkl	Key Largo Limestone	
	Qft	Fort Thompson Formation	
	Qc	Caloosahatchee Formation	
Pliocene	Pc	Citronelle Formation	Sand, gravels and clays
	Pm	Miccosukee Formation	Silty clayey quartz sands
	Pjb	Jackson Bluff Formation	Argillaceous, carbonaceous sands and shell marl
Miocene	Mchr	Charlton Formation	Phosphoritic clays and argillaceous and sandy limestones
	Mrb	Red Bay Formation	Gray sandy and clayey shell marl
	Myr	Yellow River Formation	Dark gray to bluish micaceous sands
	Mt	Tamiami Formation	Creamy white limestones, greenish gray marls, silty sands and clay
	Mbv	Bone Valley Formation	Phosphatic boulders and pebbles in matrix of phosphatic sandy clay; source of Florida's phosphate deposits
	Ma	Alachua Formation	Clay, sand, sandy clay; in Gilchrist County contains a vertebrate fauna that is one of the most prolific Miocene faunas in the U.S.
	Mfp	Fort Preston Formation	Gray and white sands; at Alum Bluff in Liberty County contains leaf impressions and carbonized logs
	Mh	Hawthorn Formation	Marine sands, clays, marls and sandy limestones; contains commercial grade attapulgite (or fullers earth)
	Msm	St. Marks Formation	Sandy chalky limestone
	Mu — Miocene undifferentiated Includes: Shoal River Formation, Chipola Formation, Chattahoochee Formation, and local exposures of the Fort Preston Formation, Hawthorn Formation, and St. Marks Formation (see above)	Shoal River Formation	Fossiliferous, micaceous, slightly clayey and silty sand
		Chipola Formation	Bluish gray to yellowish brown fossiliferous marl
		Chattahoochee Formation	Argillaceous and silty, sandy chalky limestone
Oligocene	Osi	Suwannee Limestone	Fossiliferous marine limestone
	Ou — Oligocene undifferentiated Includes: Duncan Church Beds "Byram" Formation Marianna Limestone	Duncan Church Beds	Fossiliferous shallow marine sediments consisting essentially of large foraminifers and mollusks
		"Byram" Formation	Dolomitic limestones and clays and impure limestones
		Marianna Limestone	Shallow marine granular fossiliferous limestone
Eocene	Ecr	Crystal River Formation	Shallow marine limestone composed of large foraminifers and mollusks. It is an important source of high calcium limestone and is chief supply of road stone in Florida
	Ew	Williston Formation	Shallow marine limestone, important source of road stone
	Ei	Inglis Formation	Shallow marine fossiliferous limestone and crystalline dolomite
	Eal	Avon Park Limestone	Chalky, fossiliferous limestone, and crystalline dolomite, source of dolomite limestone, agricultural stone and road stone

Oldest Rocks

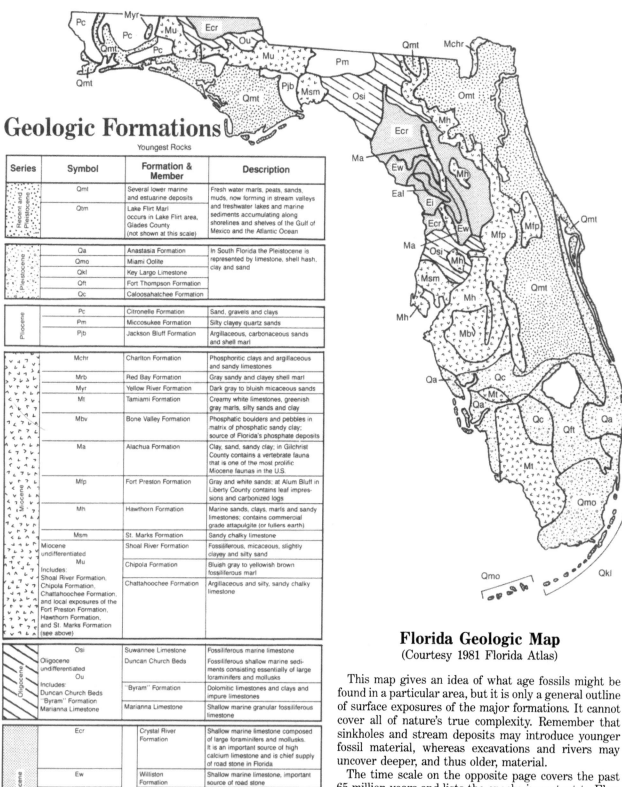

Florida Geologic Map
(Courtesy 1981 Florida Atlas)

This map gives an idea of what age fossils might be found in a particular area, but it is only a general outline of surface exposures of the major formations. It cannot cover all of nature's true complexity. Remember that sinkholes and stream deposits may introduce younger fossil material, whereas excavations and rivers may uncover deeper, and thus older, material.

The time scale on the opposite page covers the past 65 million years and lists the epochs important to Florida's fossil history. It tells you the age of the geologic formations shown on the map. This geologic time scale will be referred to frequently throughout this book.

Florida's Geologic Time-Scale

ERA	PERIOD	EPOCH		FLORIDA SURFACE FOSSIL EXPOSURES	
C E N O Z O I C	QUATERNARY	RECENT	Present to 10 thousand years ago		LAND BEGINS TO EMERGE
		PLEISTOCENE	10 thousand to 1.8 million years ago		
	TERTIARY	PLIOCENE	1.8 million to 5 million years ago		
		MIOCENE	5 million to 24.5 million years ago		
		OLIGOCENE	24.5 million to 37.5 million years ago		
		EOCENE	37.5 million to 54 million years ago		
		PALEOCENE	54 million to 65 million years ago		

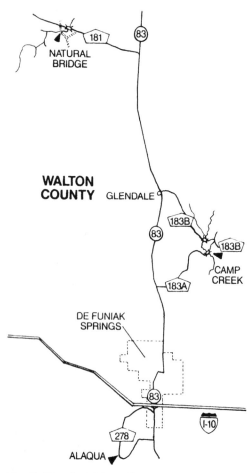

Fossil Sites in Walton County.

Accesses to the Chipola River.

stream's erosion of the Mariana Limestone. The swimming hole on the north side of the bridge is a good hunting area. Break off pieces of the upper layer of limestone and gently break into smaller pieces with a dental pick and brush to reveal the fossils.

Late Miocene shells and shell molds are exposed on a road cut near Alaqua. These mollusks are often impregnated with iron pyrites and are quite durable. They gleam with a bronze sheen. From I-10 go south on S.R. 83 about 1.6 miles and turn right on County Road 278. Follow 278 west and then north to the Alaqua Methodist Church. About .5 mile north of the church is the roadcut which exposes a lower strata of gray shale with occasional shark teeth and other marine vertebrates. The shell fossils are abundant in the red clay layer above the shale and in the interface between the two layers.

The Chipola River — In its upper reaches the Chipola is shallow enough to hunt fossils by wading and snorkeling. Pleistocene vertebrates of all kinds can be found. Look in pockets in the limestone bottom, particularly just upstream from rapids. Water is clearest in September and October. In Jackson County exit I-10 on S.R. 71 and go south less than .5 mile and turn right on S.R. 280A. Go 1.5 miles to the boat ramp at the bridge over the Chipola. The boat ramp is on the southwest side of the bridge. Wade and snorkel there or canoe up or downstream.

A second good access to the Chipola River in Jackson County is just north of Marianna. Go north on S.R. 167. About .3 mile beyond the Marianna city limits is the bridge; the boat ramp is on the southwest side. Canoe upstream and hunt as described above.

Twelve-million-year-old shells and corals, members of the Chipola Formation, crop out on the banks of the Chipola River south of Marianna. These beautifully preserved fossils were once part of a Miocene beach during a time of high sea level.

Outcrops of Chipola mollusks occur in Calhoun County. Take S.R. 20 to the Chipola River. Put in at the public ramp on the northwest side of the bridge. A canoe can usually be paddled upstream easily or you can use a small boat and outboard. The shells are found in dark gray clay on the east bank beginning about 2.5 miles upstream from the bridge. Good exposures occur opposite the mouth of Fourmile Creek and again about 4 miles further upstream opposite the mouth of Tenmile Creek.

Tenmile Creek — A wealth of Chipola shells and corals, many almost perfect, are found along the banks of this lovely creek in Calhoun County.

From S.R. 20, go north on S.R. 73 for 5.6 miles to the

Twelve-million-year-old shells from the Chipola Formation. (Photograph by Stuart Brown)

Tenmile Creek in Calhoun County.

CALHOUN COUNTY

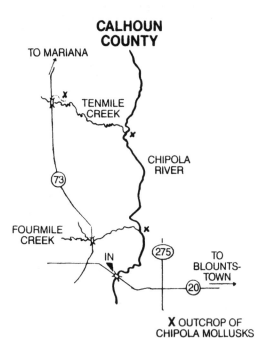

Access to Chipola River and Tenmile Creek.

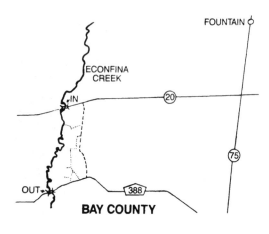

Access to Econfina Creek.

bridge over Tenmile Creek. From the northeast corner of the bridge, an unpaved road follows the stream for a short distance. The creek is shallow enough to wade for collecting. It is canoeable from the bridge to its confluence with the Chipola River, a distance of about 4 miles.

Beneath the S.R. 73 bridge, shells are found in the gray clay layer. Some shells are fragile, so collect the undisturbed clay in a bucket or plastic sack and gently extract the fossils later. Further downstream, shells are even more abundant in the reddish clay and may be collected by careful screenwashing.

Econfina Creek is really a river. It is located in Bay and Washington counties. (There is also an Econfina River which is really a creek, located in Taylor County.) The panhandle Econfina is spring-fed, clear, and fairly swift. Chipola shells are exposed along the banks and vertebrate fossils can be found on the sandy bottom in deep areas at river bends.

Because of the speed and size of the river, a float trip by canoe is best. Take S.R. 20 between Washington and Bay counties to the bridge over Econfina Creek. Put in at the northeast side of the bridge and take out at the S.R. 388 bridge, on the northwest side. Explore both the river and the spring runs that feed the Econfina. Use mask and flippers or SCUBA.

The Apalachicola River — An excellent section of panhandle geology with abundant fossil shells is located at Alum Bluff on the Apalachicola River in Liberty County. The site is owned by the Nature Conservancy and you should check in with the caretaker before visiting:

The Nature Conservancy
Northwest Florida Program
P.O. Box 393
Bristol, FL 32321
Phone: 850-643-2756

Well preserved shells and corals of the Chipola Formation are abundant in the lower strata. If you climb up the cliff you will find layers from early Miocene to recent. Occasional vertebrate fossils can be found.

Pleistocene vertebrate fossils are found on the sandbars along the Apalachicola River at times of low water level — usually fall. A good spot for sandbar hunting is downstream from the US. 90 bridge just west of Chattahoochee, Florida, in Gadsden County.

The Wacissa River in Jefferson County is clear and rather swift flowing, lined by cypress and hardwoods and fed by numerous large springs. It is extremely beautiful and quite fossiliferous, with good late Pleistocene material exposed in sandy and rocky areas along much of the bottom. A bison skull with a broken spearpoint embedded in it was found in the Wacissa, marking the site of a bison kill by paleo-Indians 11,000 years ago.

Hunting fossils with SCUBA in a spring on Econfina Creek.

The Wacissa River in Jefferson County. (Photograph by Kay Young)

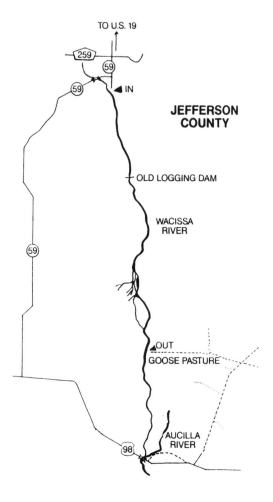

Access to Wacissa River.

A canoe is needed to reach most good fossil sites. In Jefferson County take U.S. 19 to S.R. 59 and go south to the little community of Wacissa. S.R. 59 turns right; do not turn, but continue straight about .3 mile to the recreation area on the Wacissa. Put in at the public boat ramp. Take out at Goose Pasture Park located about two miles above the junction of the Wacissa with the Aucilla. To reach Goose Pasture, take S.R. 59 west and south to U.S. 98. Turn left and go east on 98 until you cross the bridge over the Aucilla River. Take the third road on the left (it is paved for a short distance, then becomes graded limestone) and go north 4 miles to an intersection with another graded road. Turn left and go west to Goose Pasture Park.

Begin fossil hunting only after passing the old logging dam about 3 miles downstream from the put-in. Below the dam the river becomes "braided," dividing into many small channels. If you have SCUBA or are a good free diver, you can hunt in the upper parts of the braided reach where water depth is 6 to 12 feet. For snorkel and wading, go farther down the braided stretch where the water is 3 to 6 feet deep.

With a small boat and outboard you can go upstream from Goose Pasture to the lower reaches of the braided area.

The Wacissa contains a particular abundance of fossil aquatic rodents such as capybera and giant beaver.

The Aucilla River separates Jefferson County on the west from Madison and Taylor counties on the east.

The Aucilla is renowned for its elephant fossils; both mammoth and mastodon have been found in many areas. The tannin-stained brown water flows fairly slowly over sand and Ocala Limestone. Banks are wooded and in many areas covered with fern. Fossils are found in both shallow rocky stretches and deep holes at river bends. In times of low water, bones and teeth may be visible in pockets on rocks along the banks.

A good representative area can be reached in Jefferson County by taking U.S. 27 to the town of Lamont and turning south on S.R. 257. Go 7 miles to the bridge over the Aucilla. Put a canoe in on the southeast side of the bridge and float downstream about .3 mile to the first shallow area (when the water level is low, return and paddle upstream is easy). Hunt above the shallows with mask and snorkel. Look along rocks on the north bank when the water level is low. easy). Hunt above the shallows with mask and snorkel. Look along rocks on the north bank when the water level is low.

For a longer float trip, put in where U.S. 27 crosses the Aucilla at the Jefferson-Madison county line. Float down to the take-out at the S.R. 257 bridge, a distance of about 13 miles.

The Aucilla River in Taylor County.

Fossil finds laid out on the bank of the Aucilla River.

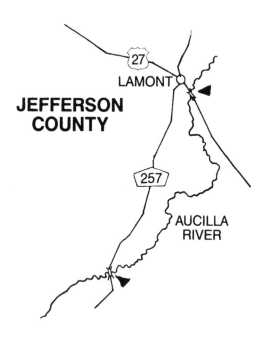

Accesses to the Aucilla River.

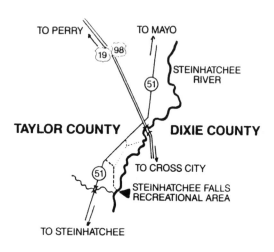

Access to Steinhatchee falls recreation area.

Beaches along the upper East Coast from the Georgia line to Cape Canaveral (Nassau to Brevard counties) present concentrations of Pleistocene seashells cemented together with limestone to form coquina rock, formerly used for building.

Just inland from the present shoreline, freshwater muck deposits often present rich samples of Pleistocene land animals.

During glacial intervals, coastal plains stretched as much as 80 miles into what is now the Atlantic Ocean, and terrestrial fossils are occasionally found on the present continental shelf. These fossils are sometimes brought in by the Atlantic surf from Fernandina to Vero Beach.

Ponte Vedra Beach in St. Johns County is just south of Jacksonville. Fossil shark teeth wash up in considerable abundance along several miles. Take S.R. A1A to Mickler Landing where there is parking and a boardwalk to the beach. You can also park along the shoulder of A1A for about six miles south of Mickler Landing. Search for shark teeth where the waves are washing up fresh material and in the shell bank higher on the beach.

The Steinhatchee River separates Taylor and Dixie counties. Its winding course through sand and limestone is interrupted by rapids and low falls. The banks are lined by huge old cypress and the surrounding land is owned by timber companies.

In shallow areas above and below rapids, holes in the bottom limestone contain gravel with a high percentage of Pleistocene land animals. Bird fossils are unusually plentiful in the Steinhatchee and mixed with the Pleistocene animals are Eocene marine fossils washed out of the Ocala Limestone through which the river flows. Teeth of ancient sharks such as *Otodus obliquus* and *Carcharodon auriculatus* often turn up, and occasionally the teeth of primitive whales called archaeocetes.

When the water level is low, bottom exposures are easy to hunt. The water is a deep brown from tannic acid, but usually not turbid. Fissures in the limestone river bed contain abundant land animal fossils. Fissures are best explored using SCUBA; deep holes may require a light. When water levels are low and the flow minimal, free diving into these fissures is possible.

In Taylor County, take U.S. 98 to state road 51. Go 2 miles south on 51 and turn left on an unpaved road. In about .3 mile the road forks; take the right fork for about 1 mile to the recreation area on a small waterfall.

Look along banks and screenwash gravel in shallows above the falls. For SCUBA hunting, canoe upstream and float back.

Quarries in Lafayette, Suwannee, Columbia, Levy,

Citrus, Marion, Alachua, and Sumter counties mine the Ocala Limestone, which is late Eocene in age. Well preserved sand dollars and sea urchins are common finds. Shells are often intact; some are present only as molds. Occasional shark teeth can be found, and rarely, one comes across the bones and teeth of ancient archaeocete whales.

Vertical sinkholes in the old limestone are often filled with orange and brown sandy clay and some contain rich accumulations of Pleistocene land animals. Several quarries are located in Lafayette County along S.R. 27, from Branford to Perry. Most have nonworking areas accessible for hunting.

The Santa Fe River, where it divides Columbia from Gilchrist and Alachua counties, contains excellent Pleistocene material and has occasional Pliocene land animal remains. Mixed with these are Eocene shark teeth. Like the Steinhatchee, the Santa Fe washes out marine fossils from the ancient Ocala Limestone over which it flows. The current is strong and water clarity is generally good from early summer to fall. Wading is possible along much of the shore and where the river passes over limestone ledges. Bottom gravel is found in pockets and contains abundant fossils. The teeth of the manatee *Trichechus,* rare elsewhere, are a common find. For strong swimmers, mask and flippers will get you into deeper areas and you can bring up gravel in fine-mesh bags. SCUBA lets you explore the deep holes.

For wading and snorkeling, the river can be reached beside the State Road 47 bridge about 6 miles south of Fort White. Park on the southeast side of the bridge. Good gravel can be found on the north bank by wading upstream from the bridge.

An excellent canoe trip begins where U.S. 27 crosses the river. Put in on the north side of the bridge and float down about 10 miles to the State Road 47 bridge. Take out on the southeast side of the bridge.

The Wacasassa River in Levy County contains good Pleistocene fossils. Put in at the S.R 24 bridge and float down to the take-out at U.S. 98 bridge. Explore the bottom for large fossils and collect gravel for screenwashing.

Accesses to the Santa Fe River.

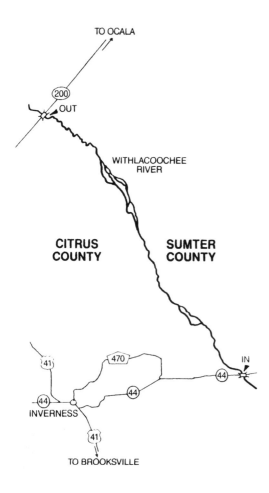

Access to the Withlacoochee River.

Central Florida

The Withlacoochee River, which divides Citrus from Marion and Sumter counties, contains Pleistocene terrestrial animals and occasional older material. A good stretch begins at the S.R. 44 bridge (put in on southeast side) to the take-out at the S.R. 200 bridge, a boat ramp on the northeast side.

Phosphate mines in Polk, Hillsborough, Hardee, Manatee, and DeSoto counties can be hunted only by scheduled field trips.

Bone Valley fossils found in phosphate mines span middle Miocene to Pliocene — some 15 million years. Both marine and terrestrial animals can be found.

South Florida

Gulf Beaches from New Port Richey to Marco Island yield occasional fossils, but beaches from Casey Key to Englewood are the most bountiful. Along this stretch, fossil shark teeth wash ashore in great numbers. Most of these are from 1/8 to 3/4 inches long, but sometimes the teeth of the giant shark *Carcharadon megalodon* can be found. Terrestrial fossils can also come ashore in this area, but in less abundance.

Search the water's edge and screen the shelly gravel where the waves are breaking. A screen of 1/4 inch hardware cloth is best. (See chapter on Equipment.) Larger fossils wash ashore after tropical storms in summer and the northwest winds that accompany cold fronts in winter.

Offshore at Venice Beach, SCUBA diving at a depth of 20 to 25 feet lets you pick up fossils before they are battered by waves. Shark teeth and good vertebrate terrestrial material are constantly being washed out of Pleistocene beds that formed when sea level was much lower than today

The Peace River, in DeSoto and Hardee counties, is shallow from October to June or July and usually clear. The bottom is composed of sand and gravel. The Peace winds through the phosphate country of Florida and contains a wealth of fossil material dating from late Miocene to Pleistocene. Banks are lined with cypress, live oak, and willow, and good campsites are plentiful. Bottom gravel contains well preserved teeth and bones. Deep holes sometimes contain large bones and the big teeth of animals such as mammoth. Fossil dugong ribs of the genus *Metaxytherium* are common finds.

Look along the edges at times of low water. Along much

Hunting fossil shells in a south Florida quarry.

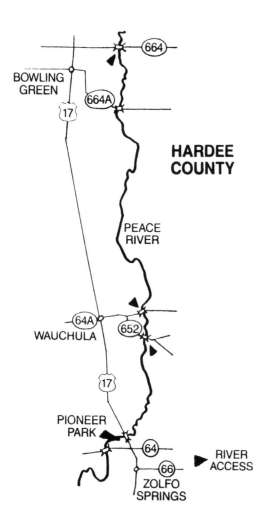

Accesses to the Peace River in Hardee County.

of its course, the river is shallow enough to wade and hunt with mask and snorkel. Any coarse gravel is worth screen-washing. Deeper holes can be easily reached with mask and fins.

Best access is by canoe. Downstream day trips or trips taking two to three days (with camping) can be arranged at a canoe livery in Arcadia.

When flow is low (October–November through June–July), it is possible to put a canoe in at public boat ramps at Arcadia, Gardener, or at the Wauchula Boat Club at Zolfo Springs. Paddle upstream and float back. The boat ramp where S.R. 70 runs parallel to the Peace River at Arcadia is also a good area for wading and snorkeling.

Joshua Creek runs into the Peace River just upstream from Nocatee on the east bank. It is reachable from the east side of the S.R. 760 bridge over the Peace River. Canoe or wade and snorkel.

Canals in Palm Beach County which are being constructed and maintained south of the town of South Bay are bordered by piles of Plio-Pleistocene shells from the Caloosahatchee, Pinecrest, and Bermont Formations. Take U.S. 27 around the southernmost tip of Lake Okeechobee, through the town of South Bay, and south for about a mile. The New River Canal runs parallel to highway 27 on the east side. On the stretch of 27 south to S.R. 827, check roads that go east, crossing the New River Canal. Look for areas of recent digging.

Limerock quarries in Charlotte, DeSoto, Glades, and Hendry counties expose the beautiful Plio-Pleisotocene shells of the Caloosahatchee Formation. Marine vertebrates such as shark teeth and whale bones are sometimes found mixed with the shells, corals, and barnacles.

Quarries in Lee and Collier counties mine the Miocene-Pliocene age shelly marls of the Tamiami Formation. Internal and external molds of 5-million-year-old mollusks and corals are remarkable for their detail. Occasionally, large and perfect mako (*Isurus hastalis*) shark teeth turn up. The younger Fort Thompson Formation overlies both the Tamiami and Caloosahatchee formations in many areas.

The Caloosahatchee River has high banks where fossils are exposed in many places, and the many creeks that empty into the Caloosahatchee in Lee and Hendry counties contain Pleistocene fossils. In creeks, look for sand

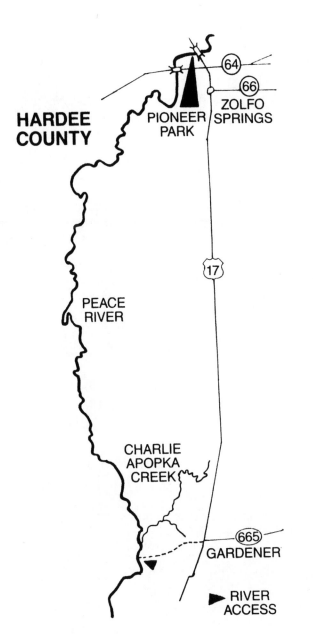

Accesses to the Peace River in
Hardee County.

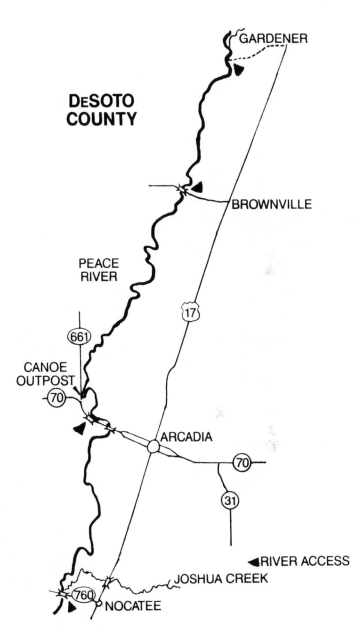

Accesses to the Peace River in
DeSoto County.

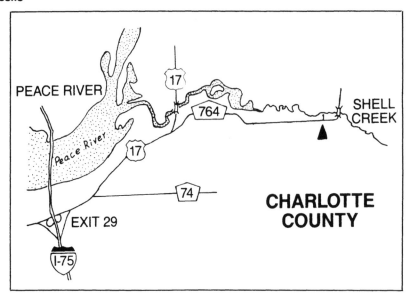

Access to Shell Creek.

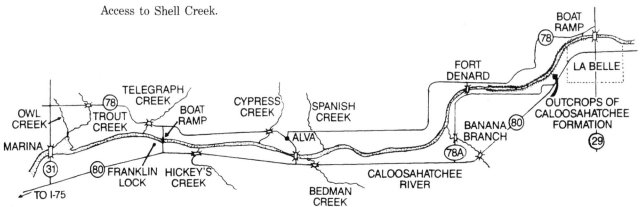

The Caloosahatchee River.

or gravel bottoms. Explore holes with mask and fins. If flow is good, organic debris on the bottom can be fanned away to expose sand and gravel.

From the Caloosahatchee River, a shallow draft boat and small outboard can get you into most of these creeks. Exit I-75 on S.R. 78 and go west to S.R. 31. Put in on the north bank of the river at the Franklin Lock in Lee County or at the public ramp on State Road 78 just west of LaBelle. Explore streams entering along one bank as you go in one direction; turn back and check the creeks on the other bank. Inspect the banks along the Caloosahatchee River as you go from creek to creek. In Hendry County, there are frequent exposures of the Caloosahatchee Formation along both banks of the river extending eastward from LaBelle for about 4 miles.

A Plio-Pleistocene "beach" — Caloosahatchee mollusks in a shell pit in Charlotte County.

Fragile fossils are wrapped in a plaster jacket for safe recovery.

Anadara rustica

CHAPTER 3

Collecting and Preserving

Most of the fossils that you find in Florida are isolated specimens — shells, bones, or teeth. Some of the oldest marine fossils, such as Eocene sea urchins, may require careful separation from the limestone in which they were deposited, but most specimens are easily freed from the matrix (sand or clay around the fossil). Many are already washed clean by rivers, surf, or rains.

You may occasionally discover an area having multiple bones, perhaps with associated teeth. This might represent the complete skeleton of a single beast. Or it could be a collection of many animals fossilized in an ancient sinkhole or stream bed. Such a find is important. It may add significantly to the knowledge of Florida's ancient past and it is likely to be of interest to those who study ancient life: the professional paleontologist.

Before you excavate further, describe what you've found to the Vertebrate Paleontology staff at the Florida Museum of Natural History in Gainesville. To make a decision about the importance of your find, an expert needs the following information:

1. A representative (but not extensive) sample of the material — a few teeth are best. But don't remove teeth if they are contained in a jaw.
2. The location of the site and a description of it: Is it in a quarry? A river bank? How close is the nearest road?
3. A sample of the matrix surrounding the fossils — shells are particularly useful — they help to establish the age of material.
4. Photographs of the site showing the fossil layer.

If timing is critical (perhaps the specimen will soon be pulverized or the site will become a housing development), call the Florida Museum of Natural History at 352-846-2000 and talk with someone in Vertebrate Paleontology. Often the find can be quickly checked by a field representative in your area. If there is no urgency, send the information to:

Vertebrate Paleontology
Florida Museum of Natural History
University of Florida
Gainesville, FL 32611

Or you may take samples to the museum and talk with the staff in person. Make an appointment first.

If the experts are interested, you are in for an exciting time working with professionals. If they are not able to use the fossils you have found, the paleontologists will courteously explain why, and will advise you on how to begin excavating them yourself.

Buried bones must be carefully uncovered before attempting removal. Toughness of fossil material varies with conditions of fossilization and how tightly the fossil is held by the surrounding matrix. Remove material from over and around the fossil with your hands or a trowel. Separate the matrix that touches the bone carefully with a brush and dental pick. Work from the specimen outward to prevent damage.

When the entire upper surface of the fossil is revealed, you will have a good idea whether it is hard enough to move without cracking or crumbling. If it seems tough, loosen the matrix below it with a trowel, remove the fossil, and wrap it in tissue or newspaper. Plastic bags of several sizes are handy for transport. If the specimen is small but has a few cracks, wrap it in aluminum foil, maintaining the orientation of fragments as much as possible. If the fossil is large and cracks badly, a plaster jacket may be needed. The next chapter, "Equipment," tells how to put together a field pack and where to find the tools and materials described in this chapter.

Plaster jackets are the paleontologist's time-honored device for getting a fragile find back to the laboratory intact. If your breakable fossil is important, a jacket may be the only way to save it. Here's how.

You will need water. If there is no close source, plan to bring a canteen or two on your jacketing trip. Other supplies you will need are a plastic pail, trowel, orthopedic plaster rolls 3 or 4 inches wide, toilet paper (for this purpose called "paleo paper"), and marking pen. If the specimen is large, a shovel will help. Burlap cut in strips and dipped in plaster of Paris is a satisfactory alternative to the orthopedic plaster.

Expose the fossil's upper surface to trace its extent. Move away from the fossil a few inches and dig a trench around it deep enough to be sure the fossil will be completely enclosed in the jacket. Undercut the fossil, leaving it perched on a pedestal of matrix. Cover exposed parts of the specimen with a 1/4-inch layer of damp toilet paper, molded to the contours. This prevents adherence between fossil and plaster. Fill any low areas in the wet paper with sand or clay. Soak the plaster bandage roll in water for a minute or two, squeeze gently, and wrap the bandage back and forth and around prepared fossil down to the pedestal, using several layers. Plaster thickness depends on jacket size, but 1/4 inch is minimum. If you are using burlap, cut strips four inches wide (feed sacks are a good source) and dip them in plaster of Paris mixed with water to the consistency of cream. Wrap the fossil as described above.

Big jackets may need additional strengthening; trim one or more small branches from a nearby tree and wrap them into the jacket, leaving ends protruding for carry-

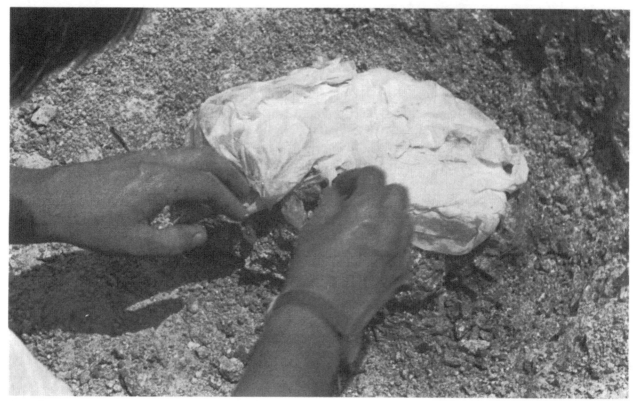

Covering the isolated specimen with toilet paper.

Dipping the plaster roll.

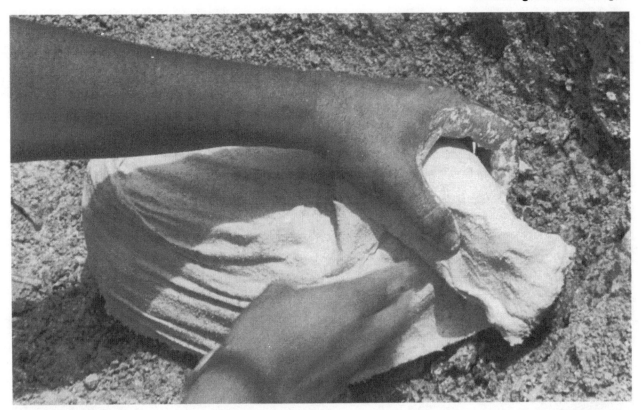

Wrapping the plaster.

Turning the jacket.

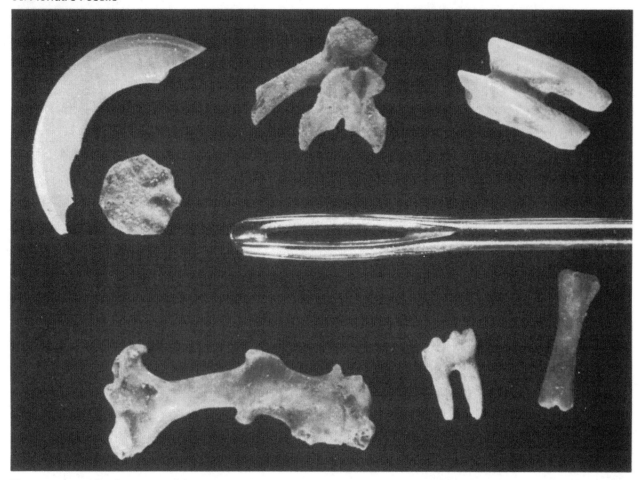

Tiny vertebrate fossils recovered by screenwashing.

ing handles. Orthopedic plaster hardens in about 20 minutes, but plaster of Paris takes about 45 minutes. When the plaster has set, use a marking pen to record the date and site, and sketch the fossil's outline on the jacket. Knowing how the specimen is oriented will help when it's time to open the jacket. Now separate the pedestal with a trowel or shovel, turn the jacket over, and wrap the bottom with plaster if needed.

Jacketing sounds elaborate but it is easier than you might think. And it is the only way to recover fragile material such as an elephant tusk or a crushed skull.

In a deposit yielding the bones of several different animals, small bones and teeth are often missed unless the material surrounding the large fossils is screenwashed. Bones and teeth of small animals such as bats, lizards, snakes, frogs, and birds can often be found by washing matrix in a wooden tray with a bottom of window screen. If a source of water is not available at the site, load some of the matrix in a tough plastic bag and take it home for screenwashing.

Many of Florida's large animal fossils are underwater finds, usually from creek or river bed. A technique of jacketing breakable specimens is also available for SCUBA fossil hunters. The submerged bones are isolated, leaving matrix around them much like beginning a plaster jacket. Three-inch-wide strips of cloth (old bed sheets are good) are wrapped around the fossil to protect it. Instead of using plaster, the jacket is made of Scotchcast — a fiberglass tape impregnated with polyurethane resin. The material comes in a waterproof foil-wrapped roll, similar to orthopedic plaster, and is used for the same purposes. Open the roll under water just before use. Wearing disposable gloves, wrap the Scotchcast around the specimen over the layer of cloth. Rolls of three- or four-inch width are best. The resin sets up 15 to 20 minutes after being exposed to water, and it forms a tough, lightweight jacket.

Before leaving the field, always make good notes and pack these data with the fossils. Use pencil or permanent marking pen. Include fossil name, formation in which it was found (if known), collector, date, and locality. When working far from roads or on rivers, a sketch map is invaluable. River sites often warrant a return visit when water levels are low or the stream is clearer. If the site is exceptional, buy a 7.5 minute topographical map or "quad sheet" of the area and mark the exact location of your find. Record this precise information with your notes on the fossils.

Preservation

At the end of a fossiling trip, nonfragile specimens should be brushed gently under running water, using a hand brush or toothbrush. Some matrix hardens with time and becomes difficult to remove. Shark teeth and many smaller vertebrate teeth often require nothing more than washing.

Fossil mollusks usually need scrubbing with a toothbrush and, when dry, a coat of clear lacquer to improve durability. The sea urchins and sand dollars from the older marine formations are sometimes more difficult to separate from their enveloping limestone. Scrape the matrix away until you can just begin to see the shell (called the test). Soak the specimen in white vinegar diluted 1:5 with water for about one minute. Then brush with a toothbrush, rinse, and soak again, until the markings on the test are clean.

Original markings on shells that seem to be featureless can sometimes be revealed under ultraviolet light. Choose cowries, cones, and olive shells. Soak the shell for three hours in laundry bleach diluted to half strength

The Eocene sea urchin *Oligopygus* as it was found and after cleaning.

with water. Rinse and dry thoroughly. Examine in a dark room under ultraviolet light. A 15-watt U.V. bulb (fluorescent fixture type) can be purchased or ordered from most lighting supply stores.

Bones or teeth in urgent need of repair can be put back together while still slightly damp, using white glue. Fragile specimens and those in plaster jackets must be dried thoroughly before cleaning. After drying, non-jacketed material can be further cleaned with an artist's brush and dental pick. Fragments are then carefully glued together with white glue (diluted with water if necessary) and applied with a fine brush. While the glue sets, fragments may be held in proper position with plasticine modeling clay.

Most fossil bones and some fossil teeth need to be hardened. The specimen must be thoroughly dry before hardener is applied. A food storage device called a "brisker" (merely a closeable metal box with a tiny heating element) makes an excellent drying cabinet for fossils.

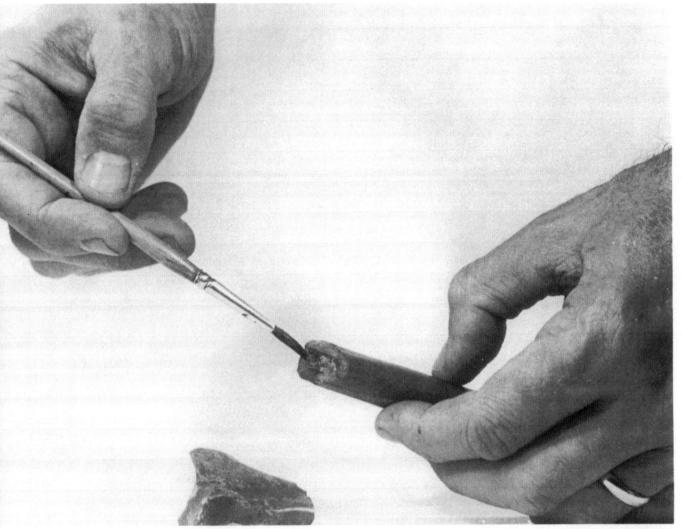

Gluing broken bone.

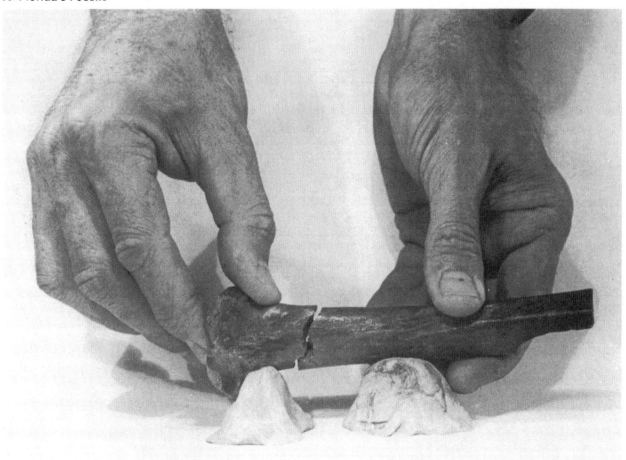

Gluing broken bone.

The hardener used by the Florida Museum of Natural History for fossil bone preservation is Butvar-76 (polyvinyl butyral) dissolved in acetone. Work in a well ventilated room. Dissolve the Butvar powder by adding it to acetone (not vice versa), to appropriate dilution. A concentrated Butvar solution makes a good bone glue: Pour while stirring, two tablespoons (30 cc) of Butvar-76 into four ounces (120 cc) of acetone. For use as bone hardener, dilute one ounce (30 cc) of the above mixture with five ounces (150 cc) of acetone.

For hardening, the dilute solution of Butvar is flowed onto the bone with a soft brush. Whitish spots on bone after applying Butvar indicate incomplete drying. The concentrated solution of Butvar makes a quick-setting bone glue for dry bone.

Completely enclosed plaster jackets are opened by sawing around the top with a small hand saw. If the interior is dry, carefully remove matrix from around the fossil with a dental pick and small brush. Harden bone fragments as needed by flowing on hardener from a brush. Never try to harden wet bone and try not to spill hardener onto adjacent matrix. Glue fragments together methodically, never removing more than one or two pieces at a time. Small gaps in a specimen can be filled with plaster of Paris and powdered papier-mache mixed in equal parts, adding enough water to make a thick paste.

Fossil finds should always be labeled with a specimen number. If the fossil is dark, apply a small patch of white acrylic paint and write the number on this. Use a fine steel penpoint or a rapidograph pen. Use waterproof ink. Keep a file of each specimen, listing name, nature of specimen (tooth, vertebrate, etc.), where found, formation, collector, and date. Files can be kept in a notebook, on three by five cards, or in a personal computer. Computer files are particularly good for large collections because they let you cross index by name, age, formation, locality, etc.

Display

Florida's wealth of fossils makes a fascinating display. When you prepare your display space, remember to allow adequate room; a single complete mammoth tooth measures twelve inches across and a Pliocene shell may stand fourteen inches tall. Include only the most perfect fossils and improve your display as you acquire better specimens.

Scientific displays may be arranged according to age, animal kinship, site of discovery, or may feature some special theme such as preservation, variation, or growth series. The Florida Museum of Natural History is a good place to see creative fossil exhibits.

Home display of vertebrate fossils. (Courtesy Ben Waller)

Fossil shells offer unique opportunities for display. For example, the Caloosahatchee mollusks found in the southern half of Florida are often more beautiful than recent beach shells. Many are minutely perfect. Most of the shells are white or cream-colored but some retain their original markings and sheen. Remarkable variation in shape exists within the same species: variation from one fossil locality to another and even among individuals at the same site. Today's shells are tantalizingly similar to these three-million-year-old mollusks and a clever display might contrast modern species with their fossil ancestors.

Always label your fossil exhibit. Include common names and scientific names wherever you can. Add additional information such as age, formation, and origin as appropriate. You can label by hand, type labels, or prepare elegant ones on slips of cardboard using press-on letters.

Small delicate fossils are shown well in compartmented boxes built to order or Riker Mounts available from biological supply houses. Casting fossils in a clear resin block makes a professional-looking display that can be handled. For flat or wall mounting, decorative mat board (used in picture framing) offers limitless colors and textures and provides a background for creative labeling and outlining.

Rare and beautiful fossils are best shown in solitary splendor. Imagine a perfect mastodon tooth in a clear glass box, illuminated from below through a white glass floor!

The fossil hunter's tools.

Dermal plate, dasyatid ray

CHAPTER 4

Equipment

Collecting fossils is a wonderfully inexpensive hobby. The fossils are there for the finding and most collecting requires simple equipment that can be easily carried. The basic items are a plastic bucket, trowel, pencil and notebook for field notes, and plastic bags. Freezer bags work well for most specimens; the tough bags in which crushed ice is sold are good for carrying matrix.

Screenwashing is a useful technique when hunting river, stream, and beach sites. Washing fossil-bearing gravels through screen mesh separates coarse materials from fine sand and clay and makes picking out the fossils much easier. You can make screenwashing boxes from materials available at a builders' supply store.

The sides are made of fir 1 x 4. The hardware cloth is held in place with 3/4-inch screen molding. For durability, use galvanized nails and cover the heads of the drywall screws with a drop of epoxy glue. It's best to have two boxes, one with coarse screen for large fossils and one with fine screen for tiny ones. The hardware cloth for the coarse box bottom should be 1/4-inch mesh. To sift out fine fossils such as miniature shells and the tiny bones and teeth of rodents, aluminum window screen which has 1/16th-inch mesh is needed. Place a layer of 1/4-inch mesh hardware cloth immediately beneath the window screen for support. The two boxes can be nested, placing the box with the coarse mesh on top. Sifting through this arrangement extracts just about everything.

Swimming fossil hunters need a mask and snorkel. In fast-moving water, fins are a necessity. A rope tied to a tree is also handy for holding position under water. Fine mesh bags with a drawstring top are useful for collecting bottom gravel and carrying small finds from deeper holes. Bags can be hand-sewn or purchased at a dive shop. Fruit or vegetable bags made of plastic net can be used for larger fossils.

A canoe opens up much more terrain. It also comfortably transports equipment and food.

On land, special finds such as fragile bones and teeth will require additional equipment.

A more complete field pack should contain:

1. Plastic bags
2. Pill vials or small zip-lock bags
3. Awl
4. Dental pick
5. Paint brushes — 1/2 and 1 inch
6. Whisk broom
7. Aluminum foil
8. Trowel
9. Pocket knife
10. Compass
11. Tissue and newspaper
12. Notebook and pencil.

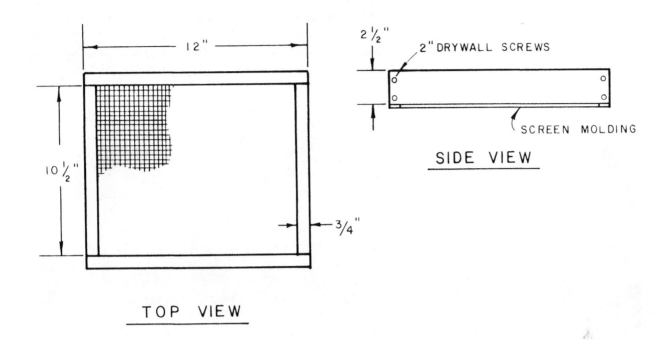

12"

10 1/2"

3/4"

TOP VIEW

2 1/2"

2" DRYWALL SCREWS

SCREEN MOLDING

SIDE VIEW

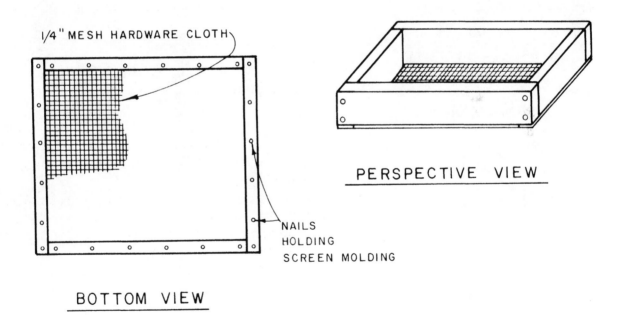

1/4" MESH HARDWARE CLOTH

NAILS
HOLDING
SCREEN MOLDING

BOTTOM VIEW

PERSPECTIVE VIEW

SCREENWASHING BOX

Tiny Plio-Pleistocene shells from the Caloosahatchee Formation recovered by screenwashing.

Making a plaster jacket will additionally require a plastic pail, rolls of plaster-impregnated gauze, and toilet paper. You may need canteens for water, and if you don't use prepared plaster rolls, take along plaster of Paris, scissors or knife, and several burlap feed sacks.

Sources for Supplies

Dental picks are really dental explorers, excavators and scalers. Ask your dental hygienist to save discarded ones for you. Or they can be ordered from Efston Science (http://www.escience.ca/hobby. The product number is 197-004).

Plaster rolls three and four inches wide can be purchased from any surgical supply store. Sometimes military surplus stores sell outdated orthopedic plaster which is still usable.

Scotchcast is the trade name of 3M's lightweight cast-making material. It consists of fiberglass tape impregnated with polyurethane resin and comes in sealed rolls, much like orthopedic plaster. The resin is catalyzed by water and sets up in 15 to 20 minutes even when immersed in a swiftly flowing river. Scotchcast is available from surgical supply stores but is expensive. Ask the orthopedic technician in your local hospital for outdated Scotchcast rolls — it has a rather short shelf life. If the roll inside the foil pouch is still soft, the material is usable.

Plastic gloves are a must when using Scotchcast. Throw-away polyethylene gloves can be purchased at most paint and hardware stores.

Plaster of Paris can be purchased at any builders' supply. Be sure that it is fast-drying and not the kind for plastering walls and ceilings!

Lacquer is available at hardware and paint stores. Dilute with acetone or lacquer thinner.

Butvar-76 (polyvinyl butyral) is available in one-pound bags from the Florida Paleontological Society. Write:

Vertebrate Paleontology
Florida Museum of Natural History
University of Florida
Gainesville, FL 32611

Dissolve by adding the powder to acetone (not vice versa), to appropriate dilution. For bone glue, pour as you stir, two tablespoons (30 cc) of Butvar-76 into four ounces (120 cc) of acetone. For use as bone hardener, dilute one ounce (30 cc) of glue with five ounces (150 cc) of acetone. Work in a well ventilated room.

Casting resin is a syrupy liquid for embedding materials in a clear plastic block. It is usually available from hobby stores.

Handbook of Paleo-preparation Techniques by Howard H. Converse is a detailed guide to all aspects of fossil preservation and display. It gives museum techniques for making exact replicas of rare finds and has an extensive list of supply sources. Price is $10.25, postage paid. Order from:

Florida Paleontological Society, Inc.
Florida Museum of Natural History
University of Florida
Gainesville, FL 32611

Papier-mache powder can be purchased from your local taxidermist.

Mat board, rub-on letters (Presstype), **pens, ink, plasticine clay, and acrylic paint** are all available from artist supply stores.

Display boxes for fossils (Riker Mounts) are shallow cardboard boxes containing cotton and having a clear plastic lid. They can be ordered from Ward's Natural Science (http://www.wardsci.com, 800-962-2660).

Detailed County Maps showing roads, parks, and other recreational features are contained in a book called *Florida County Maps and Recreational Guide,* available at most Florida bookstores.

Topographical Maps of Florida prepared by the United States Geological Survey which are large-scaled and highly detailed (scale 7-1/2 minute–also called "quad sheets") are available from the USGS web site: http://www.usgs.gov.

A screenful of gravel from the Steinhatchee River.

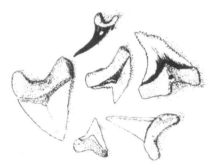

Shark teeth

CHAPTER 5

Identifying the Fossils You Find

Fossil Names

Some fossil animals were much like their living descendants. The alligator (*Alligator mississippiensis*) hasn't changed much from its 18-million-year-old ancestor (*Alligator olseni*), which has been unearthed at the Thomas Farm bone bed in North Florida. But other extinct animals were so different from today's beasts that it is not possible to attach a common name to them. An extinct carnivore, also known from Thomas Farm, was similar to both the extinct hyenoid (bone-crushing) dogs and the living wolves, but can't truthfully be called either one. The fossil hunter's enthusiasm for a new find might be damped by having to shout, "I've just found part of a Miocene carnivore intermediate in development between the wolf and the hyenoid dogs!" Simply shouting *"Tomarctus!"* says it all. Common everyday names won't work — most fossil beasts just don't have them.

Binomial nomenclature is the two-name system used by scientists around the world for identifying an organism. Creatures having the closest similarities to one another are grouped together to form a **species**. Species that resemble each other are grouped to form a **genus**. Generic names are capitalized and species names are not; both names are italicized. Most names come from Greek or Latin words; some are names of people or places.

Animals are further grouped into broader categories. Similar genera are assigned to a family, families to an order, orders to a class, classes to a phylum, and phyla to a kingdom. Using these categories is like playing the game "twenty questions," starting with animal or vegetable, then going on to describe the creature with increasing exactness. The full name of the domestic cat, for instance, would be:

Kingdom — Animalia
Phylum — Chordata
Class — Mammalia
Order — Carnivora
Family — Felidae
Genus — *Felis*
Species — *domestica*

From now on in this book, genus (and when possible, species) names are given. The common name is listed if there is one. When the names of larger groupings such as family or order are used, common names are given too. But try to develop a familiarity with the scientific names. For future reading about fossils it is convenient to know, without having to look it up, that the order Proboscidea is made up of elephants and related animals.

How to Tell It's a Fossil

Sometimes a specimen may look suspiciously like a bone or tooth of a recent animal. This is particularly true of river-bottom finds. One way to help decide is to apply flame to the bone; if it smells like burning hair, it still contains protein and is recent, not fossil. And some fossil bone has a china-like "chink" when tapped.

Many fossil teeth are virtually unaltered from their original state. Minerals *may* be deposited in fossil bone; in Florida these minerals include carbonates and silicates. Some Pleistocene bone is altered very little. Color and hardness are not reliable indicators of age. Both are the result of chemical conditions immediately surrounding the fossil.

But as a general rule, age can best be determined by knowledge about the fossil animal and when it lived. Additional clues are often gained from the layer or formation in which it was found.

Fossils that Indicate Age

Some of Florida's fossil vertebrates became extinct after a relatively short timespan and thus serve as good indicators of age. For instance, if there are rhino teeth in a layer with other fossils, it's likely the deposit is at least four million years old. Rhinoceroses became extinct in Florida about four million years ago.

The following list of genera gives some common vertebrate time indicators. If the species name of the fossil is also known, even more precise age reckoning can be made. (For a more extensive table of ages of Florida land mammals, see Appendix D.)

Name	Time in Years Before Present
1. *Bison* ("buffalo")	.5 million or less
2. *Mammuthus* (mammoth)	10,000 to 1.5 million
3. *Equus* (modern horse)	10,000 to 4 million
4. *Mammut* (mastodon)	10,000 to 4 million
5. *Teleoceras* and *Aphelops* (rhinoceros)	4 million to 10 million

What About Carbon 14 Dating?

Radiocarbon is widely used to determine the ages of fossils from the late Pleistocene. Carbon 14 is a radioactive isotope which is constantly being produced in the upper atmosphere by cosmic radiation of carbon 12 in carbon dioxide. So a constant percentage of radiocarbon is present in the environment of every living organism, and plants and animals continually incorporate the isotope

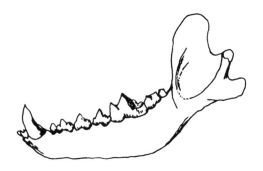

Carnivore lower jaw (wolf).

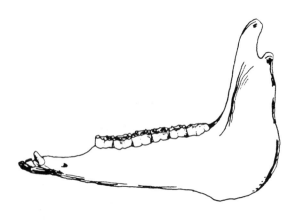

Herbivore lower jaw (horse).

into their tissues. While alive, an organism contains a constant fraction of carbon 14. When the organism dies, it ceases to take up radiocarbon and the carbon 14 atoms present diminish by radioactive decay at a predictable rate. Thus by measuring the amount of carbon 14 remaining in fossil bone, its age can be determined. But accuracy is limited to about 60,000 years — only about 0.1% of the time spanned by Florida's fossil history. The test now costs about $375 and it may require the destruction of a considerable amount of fossil specimen. Accelerator mass spectrometry (AMS) can establish carbon 14 age with as little as one gram of specimen. Its cost is about $600. Neither method is likely to be very helpful to amateur paleontologists.

Fossil Teeth

The hardest parts of vertebrate animals are their teeth. For this reason, teeth are most likely to fossilize. Teeth are especially informative fossils because they have characteristic features peculiar to each animal. Many species of vertebrates can be identified from a single tooth. The shape and number of teeth also can provide good information about the diet of an extinct animal. Among the mammals, the meat-eaters (carnivores) have long, tearing or piercing canines and a specialized set of cheek teeth called carnassials that are modified for cutting and shearing. The grass-eaters (herbivores) often have flattened incisors for cropping and their molars have a large surface area for crushing and grinding. Omnivores, such as man, have modifications of both patterns and can eat a variety of foods.

Bony Armor

Armadillos and related beasts called glyptodonts had bony plates beneath the skin which acted as protective armor. These plates are often fossilized. Each has a characteristic pattern of surface and edge markings that tells from which animal it came.

The backs of alligators and crocodiles had rows of bony plates called osteoderms located just beneath the skin. Osteoderms are roughly square and pitted and are common fossil finds.

Turtle shells break down into individual plates called scutes. The shape and surface pattern of a scute identifies the kind of turtle from which it came.

Modern Skeletons

Familiarity with the appearance of the bones of several animals living in Florida today can help a lot in identifying vertebrate fossils. Modern deer, horse, bobcat, raccoon, opossum, rabbit, and cotton rat all closely resemble their Pleistocene counterparts. The bony armor of today's common armadillo, *Dasypus novemcinctus*, reproduces in miniature the bony plates of *Dasypus bellus* from the Pleistocene. Fossil wolf bones look much like the bones of a large modern dog, and extinct bison bones look a lot like the parts of a large cow. A bone collection gathered from road kills and skeletons found in the woods is a great aid in "keying out" fossil bones and teeth not shown in the identification section of this book.

Sharks

Shark skeletons are made of cartilage which doesn't fossilize. Their vertebrae sometimes become calcified and wind up as fossils. But their teeth are the most abundant marine vertebrate fossil in Florida. The living lemon shark, *Negaprion brevirostris* (also abundant in the fossil record) is a good example of why so many shark teeth are found. A lemon shark's teeth are produced in 6 to 7 parallel rows and are loosely anchored in the jaw. Teeth fall out easily and new teeth are constantly being made. There are about 64 mature teeth in place all the time. Replacement time for lost teeth is about 8 days. So in a single year this shark could produce 3,000 teeth! A mammal, by contrast, produces at most 60 to 70 teeth in a lifetime.

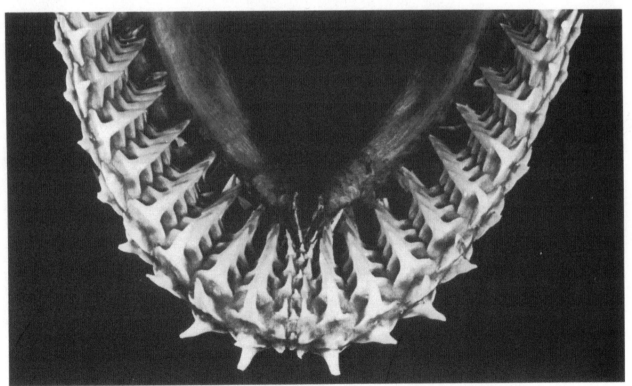

The jaw of a modern lemon shark *Negaprion brevirostris*. (Courtesy Zooarcheology, Florida Museum of Natural History)

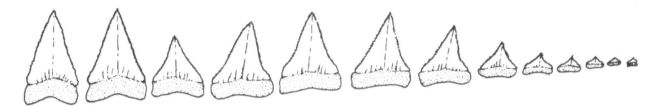

Half of the upper teeth of the modern great white shark *(Carcharodon carcharias)* to show size and shape variation. The largest teeth are in the front of the mouth.

Shark teeth often differ in size and shape between the upper and lower jaw and even from front to back in the same jaw.

The size of fossil teeth found in Florida varies from the tiny teeth of the sharpnosed shark *Rhizoprionodon* (only collected by screenwashing), to the four-inch giants of the extinct giant white shark, *Carcharodon megalodon.*

Carcharodon megalodon has had a lot written about it, much of which is pure speculation. But the known facts are fascinating enough. Teeth do reach six or seven inches in size and the animal certainly grew to 50 feet in length and perhaps larger. It appeared in the Miocene and was the immediate ancestor of *Carcharodon carcharias,* the modern great white shark. The teeth of *C. megalodon* and *C. carcharias* are quite similar. In Florida, *C. megalodon* teeth are found in deposits of Miocene through Pleistocene age.

Rays

The skeletons of rays are also made of cartilage and do not fossilize, but ray grinding or "pavement" teeth, dermal plates, and barbed tail spines are common fossils.

The Time Scale

For each specimen identified, the approximate time when the animal lived is indicated by a time unit. These units are divisions of the last 65 million years, an interval called the Cenozoic Era. Units of the Cenozoic are called epochs; each epoch spans a few hundred thousand to several million years. The time chart of the Cenozoic is presented again; it will help tell you how old your fossil find is.

Florida's Geologic Time-Scale

ERA	PERIOD	EPOCH			
C E N O Z O I C	QUATERNARY	RECENT	Present to 10 thousand years ago	F L O R I D A S U R F A C E F O S S I L E X P O S U R E S	
		PLEISTOCENE	10 thousand to 1.8 million years ago		
	TERTIARY	PLIOCENE	1.8 million to 5 million years ago		LAND BEGINS TO EMERGE
		MIOCENE	5 million to 24.5 million years ago		
		OLIGOCENE	24.5 million to 37.5 million years ago		
		EOCENE	37.5 million to 54 million years ago		
		PALEOCENE	54 million to 65 million years ago		

Identifying Florida Fossils

The following photographs and drawings illustrate many of the fossils found in Florida. Scientific and (when possible) common names are listed, and pointers on characteristic features are offered. Specimens photographed from the collections of the Florida Museum of Natural History are noted FSM (formerly Florida State Museum).

PLATE 1
Invertebrates
(corals, mollusks, barnacles, echinoids, and crabs)

Phylum Coelenterata

Class Anthozoa (**corals**)

> Miocene Coral from the Chipola Formation —
> about 13 million years old

Order Scleractinia

Family Faviidae
A. *Antillophyllia chipolana* Weisbord — 3/4 x 1⅝ inches (2 x 4 cm) Bay County — extinct

> Plio-Pleistocene Corals from the Caloosahatchee Formation — about three million years old

Order Scleractinia

Family Faviidae
B. *Manicina areolata* (Linne) — 4 x 1½ inches (10 x 3.5 cm) Hendry County

C. *Solenastrea bournoni* Edwards and Haime — 3½ x 2½ inches (7.5 x 6.5 cm) Hendry County

Family Meandrinidae
D. *Dichocoenia caloosahatcheensis* Weisbord — 5⅛ x 4¾ inches (13 x 12 cm) Hendry County — extinct

Family Siderastreidae
E. *Siderastrea dalli* Vaughan — 2⅜ x 2⅜ inches (6 x 6 cm) Hendry County — extinct

Family Rhizangiidae
F. *Oculina diffusa* Lamarck — 1 ⅛ x 3/4 inches (3 x 2 cm) Hendry County

PLATE 1   Identifying the Fossils You Find/79

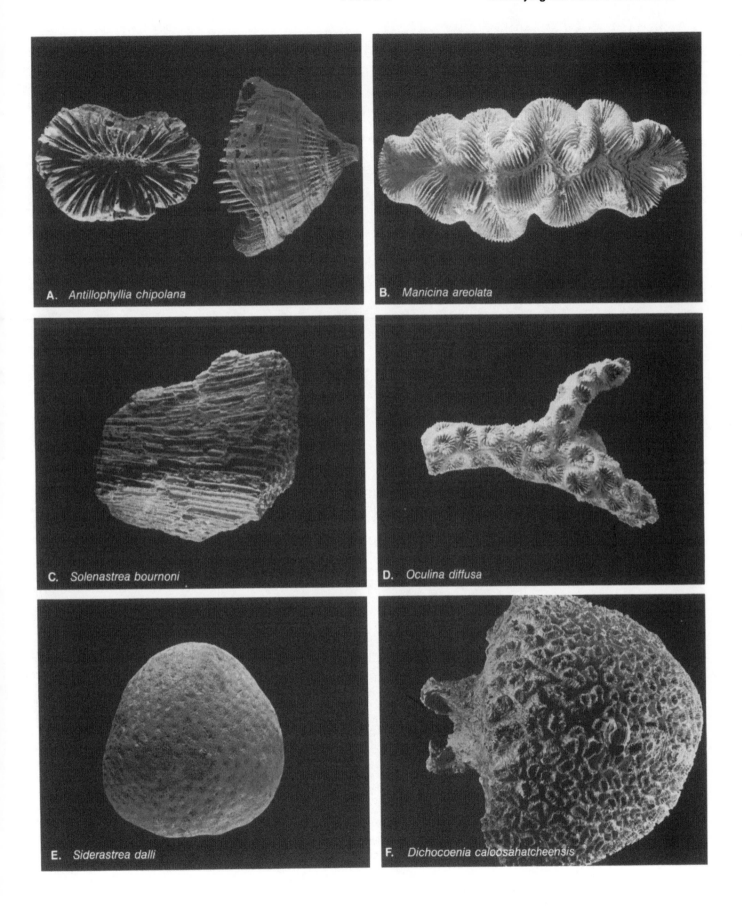

A. *Antillophyllia chipolana*

B. *Manicina areolata*

C. *Solenastrea bournoni*

D. *Oculina diffusa*

E. *Siderastrea dalli*

F. *Dichocoenia caloosahatcheensis*

PLATE 2

Phylum Mollusca (**shells**)

> Eocene Mollusks from the Ocala Limestone.
> These mollusks are about 45 million years old.
> Most are found as internal or external molds.
> Some pectens (**scallop shells**) survive intact.

Class Gastropoda

Order Mesogastropoda

Family Architectonicadae
A. *Architectonica* and other mollusks in the Ocala Limestone — 5 x 3½ inches (13 x 9 cm) overall   Sumter County — extinct (FSM)

Order Veneroida

Family Cardiidae
B. *Trachycardium* internal mold in Ocala Limestone — 1⅝ x 1½ inches (4.3 x 4 cm)   Lafayette County — extinct (FSM)

> Oligocene from the Suwannee Limestone.
> Suwannee shells are 25 to 37 million years old
> and preservation is similar to the Eocene
> mollusks.

Order Mesogastropoda

Family Xenophoridae
C. *Xenophora* internal mold in Suwannee Limestone — 6 x 3½ inches (15 x 9 cm) overall   Hernando County — extinct (FSM). This is an inside mold of the "carrier shell" shown in Plate 8, photograph D.

> Miocene from the Chipola Formation. Chipola
> mollusks are about 13 million years old.
> Despite their age, most are beautifully
> preserved.

Class Gastropoda

Order Mesogastropoda

Family Cassidae
D. *Semicassis aldrichi* (Dall) — 1¾ x 1⅜ inches (4.5 x 3 cm) Calhoun County — extinct (FSM)

Family Strombidae
E. *Orthaulax gabbi* Dall — 1½ x 1/2 inches (4 x 2 cm)   Calhoun County — extinct (FSM)

Class Bivalvia

Order Ostreoida

Family Pectinidae
F. *Nodipecten condylomatus* (Dall) — 1⅝ x 1⅛ inches (4 x 3 cm)   Calhoun County — extinct (FSM)

PLATE 2   **Identifying the Fossils You Find**/81

A. *Architectonica* internal mold

B. *Trachycardium* internal mold

C. *Xenophora* internal mold

D. *Semicassis aldrichi*

E. *Orthaulax gabbi*

F. *Nodipecten condylomatus*

PLATE 3

Order Veneroida

Family Veneridae
A. *Chione chipolana* Dall — 1/2 x 1/2 inch (1.5 x 1.5 cm) Calhoun County — extinct (FSM)

  Miocene-Pliocene from the Tamiami Formation. These mollusks are about two to five million years old. Most remain only as molds, but pectens and oyster shells are found intact.

B. Internal molds of several Tamiami mollusks — largest 2 x 1¾ inches (5.5 x 4.4 cm) Lee County

  Miocene-Pliocene from the Pinecrest Formation. Pinecrest shells are probably the same age as Tamiami mollusks, but they are preserved intact.

Class Bivalvia

Order Veneroida

Family Veneridae
C. *Chione propeulocyma* Mansfield — 1¾ x 1⅜ inches (4.5 x 3 cm) Sarasota County — extinct (FSM)

Family Tellinidae
D. *Tellidora lunulata* Holmes — 1⅜ x 1⅛ inches (3.5 x 2.8 cm) Sarasota County (FSM)

Class Gastropoda

Order Neogastropoda

Family Terebridae
E. *Terebra unilineata* Conrad — 5½ x 3/4 inches (14 x 2 cm) Sarasota County — extinct (FSM)

Family Melongenidae
F. *Busycon echinatum* (Dall) — 2⅜ x 1⅛ inches (6 x 3 cm) Sarasota County — extinct (FSM)

PLATE 3   **Identifying the Fossils You Find**/83

A. *Chione chipolana*

B. Internal molds of Tamiami shells

C. *Chione propeulocyma*

D. *Tellidora lunulata*

E. *Terebra unilineata*

F. *Busycon echinatum*

PLATE 4

Family Muricidae
A. *Ecphora quadricostata* (Say) — 3½ x 3⅛ inches (9 x 8 cm) Sarasota County — extinct (FSM). This shell is an important indicator of the Miocene.

Plio-Pleistocene from the Caloosahatchee Formation. Caloosahatchee shells are about one to three million years old and their state of preservation is superb.

Class Bivalvia (bivalves)

Order Arcoida

Family Arcidae
B. *Arca wagneriana* Dall — 5 x 2 inches (13 x 5 cm)   Hendry County — extinct

C. *Anadara rustica* (Tuomey and Holmes) — 2 x 1⅜ inches (5.5 x 5.5 cm)   Hendry County — extinct

Order Ostreoida

Family Pectinidae
D. *Lyropecten nodosus* (Linne) — 4 x 3½ inches (10 x 9 cm) Hendry County — extinct

Family Spondylidae
E. *Spondylus rotundatus* Heilprin — 2½ x 2 inches (6.5 x 5 cm) Hendry County — extinct

Order Hippuritoida

Family Chamidae
F. *Arcinella arcinella* (Linne) — 1¾ x 1⅝ inches (4.5 x 4 cm) Sarasota County

PLATE 4   **Identifying the Fossils You Find**/85

A. *Ecphora quadricostata*

B. *Arca wagneriana*

C. *Anadara rustica*

D. *Lyropecten nodosus*

E. *Spondylus rotundatus*

F. *Arcinella arcinella*

PLATE 5

Order Veneroida

Family Cardiidae
A. *Cardium dalli* Heilprin — 5 x 3½ inches (13 x 9 cm) Hendry
County — extinct

Family Veneridae
B. *Chione cancellata* (Linne) — 1½ x 1½ inches (3.3 x 3.3 cm)
Hendry County

C. *Chione latilirata* (Conrad) — 1⅛ x 3/4 inches (2.7 x 2 cm)
Hendry County

Order Neogastropoda

Family Conidae
D. *Conus adversarius tryoni* Heilprin — 4 x 1¾ inches (10 x 4.5
cm) Hendry County — extinct

Family Cancellariidae
E. *Cancellaria conradiana* Dall — 1¾ x 1 inches (4.5 x 2.5 cm)
Hendry County

F. *Trigonostoma sericea* Dall — 3/4 x 1/2 inch (2 x 1.5 cm) Hendry
County — extinct

PLATE 5   **Identifying the Fossils You Find**/87

A. *Cardium dalli*

B. *Chione cancellata*

C. *Chione latilirata*

D. *Conus adversarius tryoni*

E. *Cancellaria conradiana*

F. *Trigonostoma sericea*

PLATE 6

Family Turbinellidae
A. *Turbinella regina* (Heilprin) — 8 x 2¾ inches (20 x 7 cm)
Hendry County — extinct

B. *Vasum horridum* Heilprin — 3½ x 2 inches (9 x 5 cm) Hendry
County — extinct

Family Mitridae
C. *Mitra heilprini* Cossman — 2⅜ x 1/2 inches (6 x 1.4 cm)
Hendry County — extinct

Family Volutidae
D. *Scaphella floridana* (Heilprin) — 5 x 2 inches (12.5 x 5 cm)
Hendry County — extinct

Family Melongenidae
E. *Busycon rapum* (Heilprin) — 3¾ x 1¾ inches (9.5 x 4.5 cm)
Hendry County — extinct

Family Fasciolariidae
F. *Fasciolaria scalarina* Heilprin — 6¼ x 2¾ inches (16 x 7 cm)
Hendry County — extinct

PLATE 6   Identifying the Fossils You Find/89

A. *Turbinella regina*

B. *Vasum horridum*

C. *Mitra heilprini*

D. *Scaphella floridana*

E. *Busycon rapum*

F. *Fasciolaria scalarina*

PLATE 7

A. *Liochlamys bulbosa* (Heilprin) — 2½ x 1⅝ inches (6.5 x 4 cm)
Hendry County — extinct

Family Fusidae
B. *Fusinus caloosaensis* Heilprin — 3⅛ x 1 inches (8 x 2.5 cm)
Hendry County — extinct

Family Buccinidae
C. *Hanetia mengeana* Heilprin — 3/4 x 5/8 inch (2 x 1.5 cm)
Hendry County — extinct

Family Muricidae
D. *Chicoreus brevifrons* (Dall) — 1⅛ x 1⅛ inches (3 x 3 cm)
Hendry County

E. *Phyllonotus pomum* (Gmelin) — 3½ x 2½ inches (9 x 6 cm)
Hendry County

Order Mesogastropoda

Family Cypreaidae
F. *Cypraea problematica* (Heilprin) — dorsal view — 2¾ x 1¾
inches (7 x 4.5 cm) Hendry County

PLATE 7   **Identifying the Fossils You Find**/91

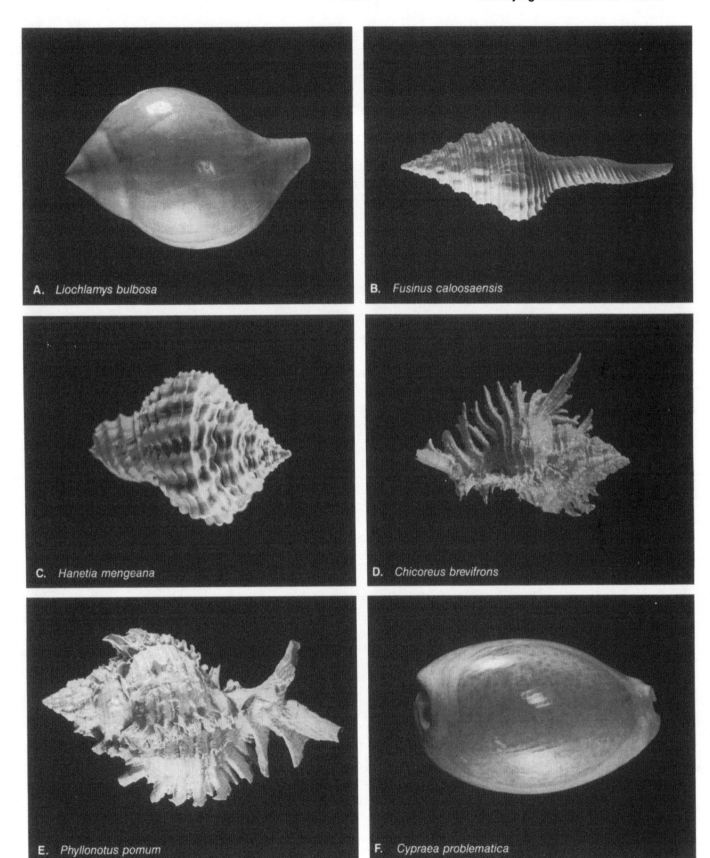

A. *Liochlamys bulbosa*

B. *Fusinus caloosaensis*

C. *Hanetia mengeana*

D. *Chicoreus brevifrons*

E. *Phyllonotus pomum*

F. *Cypraea problematica*

PLATE 8

A. *Cypraea problematica* (Heilprin) — apertural view — 2¾ x 1¾ inches (7 x 4.5 cm) Hendry County — extinct

Family Strombidae
B. *Strombus leidyi* Heilprin — 8 x 5 inches (20 x 12.5 cm) Hendry County — extinct

C. *Strombus pugilis* Lenne — 4 x 2 inches (10 x 5 cm) Hendry County

Family Xenophoridae
D. *Xenophora conchyliophora* (Born) — 1⅜ x 1⅛ inches (3.5 x 3 cm) Hendry County

Family Turritellidae
E. *Vermicularia recta* Olsson and Harbison — 12 x 3½ inches (30 x 9 cm) Hendry County — extinct

F. *Turritella perattenuata* Heilprin — 2½ x 3/4 inches (6.5 x 1 cm) Hendry County — extinct

PLATE 8   **Identifying the Fossils You Find**/93

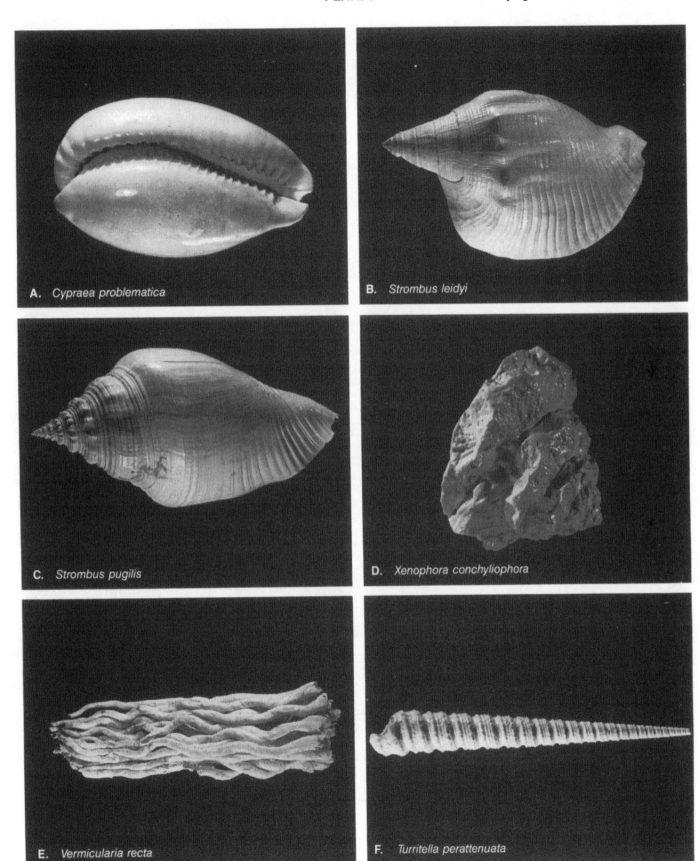

A. *Cypraea problematica*

B. *Strombus leidyi*

C. *Strombus pugilis*

D. *Xenophora conchyliophora*

E. *Vermicularia recta*

F. *Turritella perattenuata*

PLATE 9

Family Melanellidae
A. *Niso willcoxiana* Dall — 1⅛ x 1/2 inches (3 x 1.2 cm)   Hendry County — extinct

Order Bassommatophora

Family Physidae
B. *Stenophysa meigsii* (Dall) — 1/2 x 3/8 inch (1.5 x 1 cm) Hendry County — extinct

Phylum Echinodermata (**sand dollars, sea biscuits, sea urchins and sea stars**)

Eocene Echinoids from the Ocala Limestone

Class Echinoidea

Order Spatangoida

Family Brissidae
C. *Eupatagus antillarum* (Cotteau) — 2⅜ x 1¾ inches (6 x 4.5 cm)   Lafayette County — extinct (FSM)

Family Schizasteridae
D. *Schizaster armiger* (Clark) — 2⅜ x 2⅛ inches (6 x 5.5 cm) Lafayette County — extinct (FSM)

Order Holectypoida

Family Olygopygidae
E. *Oligopygus wetherbyi* de Loriol — 1¾ x 1⅜ inches (4.5 x 3.5 cm)   Lafayette County — extinct (FSM)

Order Clypeasteroida

Family Neolaganidae
F. *Weisbordella cubae* (Weisbord) — 1 x 3/4 inch (3 x 2 cm) Lafayette County — extinct (FSM)

PLATE 9   **Identifying the Fossils You Find**/95

A. *Niso willcoxiana*

B. *Stenophysa meigsii*

C. *Eupatagus antillarum*

D. *Schizaster armiger*

E. *Oligopygus wetherbyi*

F. *Weisbordella cubae*

PLATE 10

Oligocene Echinoids from the Suwannee
Limestone

Order Cassiduloida

Family Cassidulidae
A. *Rhyncholampas gouldii* (Bouve) — 1½ x 1½ inches (4 x 4 cm)
Suwannee County — extinct (FSM)

Miocene-Pliocene Echinoids from the Tamiami
Formation

Order Clypeasteroida

Family Mellitidae
B. *Encope tamiamiensis* Mansfield — 1⅝ x 1⅜ inches (4 x 3.5
cm)   Collier County — extinct (FSM)

Plio-Pleistocene Echinoids from the
Caloosahatchee Formation

Order Clypeasteroidea

Family Clypeasteridae
C. *Clypeaster rosaceus* (Linne) — 4 x 3½ inches (1.5 x 8.5 cm)
Hendry County

Class Cirripedia (**barnacles**)

Miocene-Pliocene from the Tamiami Formation

Order Thoracica

Family Balanidae
D. *Balanus* — 1¾ x 1⅝ inches (4.5 x 4 cm)   Hendry County

Class Malacostraca (**crabs**)

Order Decapoda

Family Diogenidae
E. Fragments of crab shells, mostly hermit crab, *Petrochirus* —
largest 1 inch (2.5 cm)   Lee County — Pliocene

Vertebrate Fossils

Phylum Chordata

Class Chondrichthyes (**the "cartilage fish" — sharks, skates,
and rays**)

Shark Teeth

Order Selachii

Family Orectolobidae
F. *Ginglymostoma* — **nurse sharks** — 3/4 x 5/16 inches (1.8 x 1.4
cm)   Columbia County — Oligocene to Recent (FSM)

PLATE 10   Identifying the Fossils You Find/97

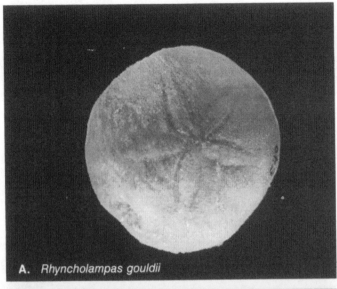

A. *Rhyncholampas gouldii*

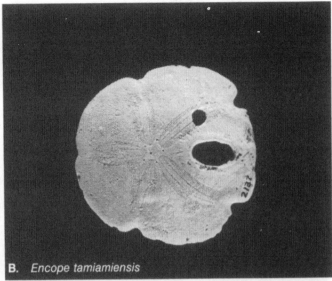

B. *Encope tamiamiensis*

C. *Clypeaster rosaceus*

D. *Balanus*

E. Fragments of crab shells

F. Nurse shark tooth

PLATE 11

Family Odontaspidae
A. *Odontaspis cuspidata* — **extinct sand shark** — 1½ x 3/4
inches (4 x 2 cm) Lee County — Oligocene to Miocene.
O. cuspidata is difficult to distinguish from *Odontaspis taurus,*
the **sand tiger shark**, which spans Miocene to Recent.

Family Isuridae
B. *Otodus obliquus* — **extinct mackerel shark** — 7/8 x 3/4 inch
(2.3 x 2 cm) Gilchrist County — Eocene to Oligocene

C. *Carcharodon carcharias* — **great white shark** — 1⅝ x 1¼
inches (4 x 3.3 cm) Charlotte County — Pleistocene to
Recent

D. *Carcharodon megalodon* — **extinct giant white shark** — 2 x
1⅝ inches (5 x 4 cm) DeSoto County — Miocene to
Pleistocene

E. *Carcharodon auriculatus* — **extinct giant white shark** — 2 x
1¾ inches (5 x 4.5 cm) Polk County — Eocene to Miocene
(FSM)

F. *Isurus hastalis* — **extinct mako shark** — upper 1⅜ x 1⅜
inches (4.5 x 3.5 cm) and lower 1⅜ x 1⅛ inches (4.5 x 2.8
cm) Polk County — Miocene to Pliocene (FSM). *Isurus,*
Hemipristis, and *Carcharinus,* have lower teeth that are
narrower than the upper teeth.

PLATE 11   Identifying the Fossils You Find/99

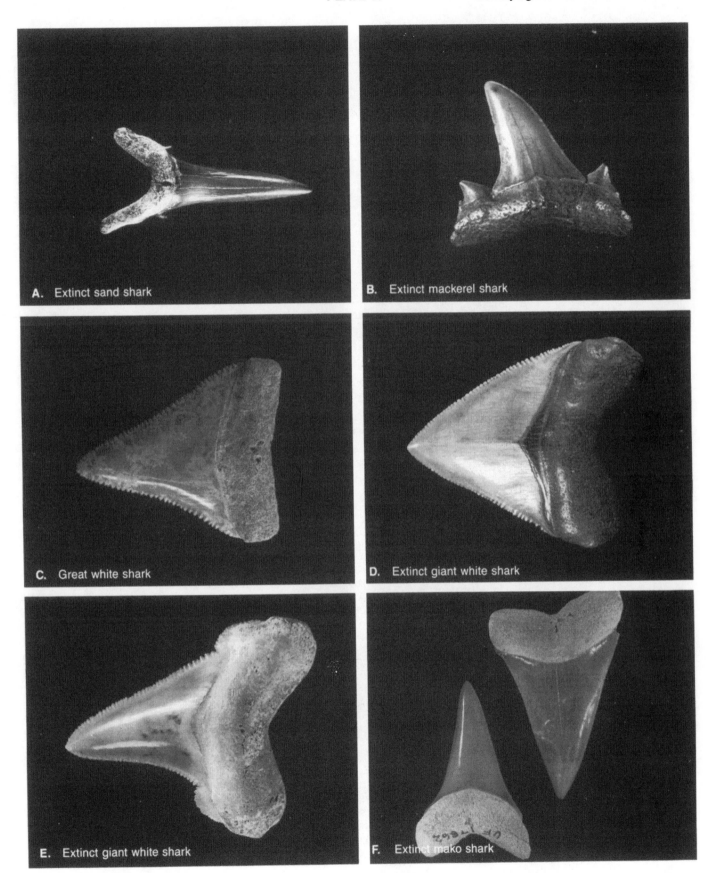

A. Extinct sand shark

B. Extinct mackerel shark

C. Great white shark

D. Extinct giant white shark

E. Extinct giant white shark

F. Extinct mako shark

PLATE 12

Family Carcharhinidae (**the requiem sharks**)

A. *Galeocerdo cuvieri* (right) **tiger shark** — 1⅛ x 1⅛ inches (3 x 2.8 cm) Lee County — Miocene to Recent and *Galeocerdo aduncas* (left) **extinct tiger shark** Alachua County — Miocene to Pliocene (FSM)

B. *Hemipristis serra* — **extinct snaggletooth shark** — upper 1⅛ x 1 inch (3 x 2.5 cm) and lower 1⅜ x 3/4 inches (3.5 x 2 cm) Hardee County — Miocene to Pliocene (FSM)

C. *Negaprion brevirostris* — **lemon shark** — 7/8 x 3/4 inch (2.2 x 2 cm) Lee County — Oligocene to Recent

D. *Rhizoprionodon terrae-novae* — **sharp-nosed shark** — 3/16 x 1/8 inch (.5 x .3 cm) Lee County — Oligocene to Recent. These tiny shark teeth are only found by screenwashing.

E. *Carcharhinus* species — upper 1 x 3/4 inches (2.5 x 2 cm) and lower 3/4 x 1/2 inch (2 x 1.5 cm) Polk County (FSM). Three species of *Carcharhinus* are difficult to distinguish from one another: *Carcharhinus leucas* (**bull shark**), *Carcharhinus obscurus* (**dusky shark**), and *Carcharhinus limbatus* (**small black-tipped shark**), all Miocene to Recent.

F. Shark vertebra — 1¼ x 1⅛ inches (3.3 x 3 cm) Lee County

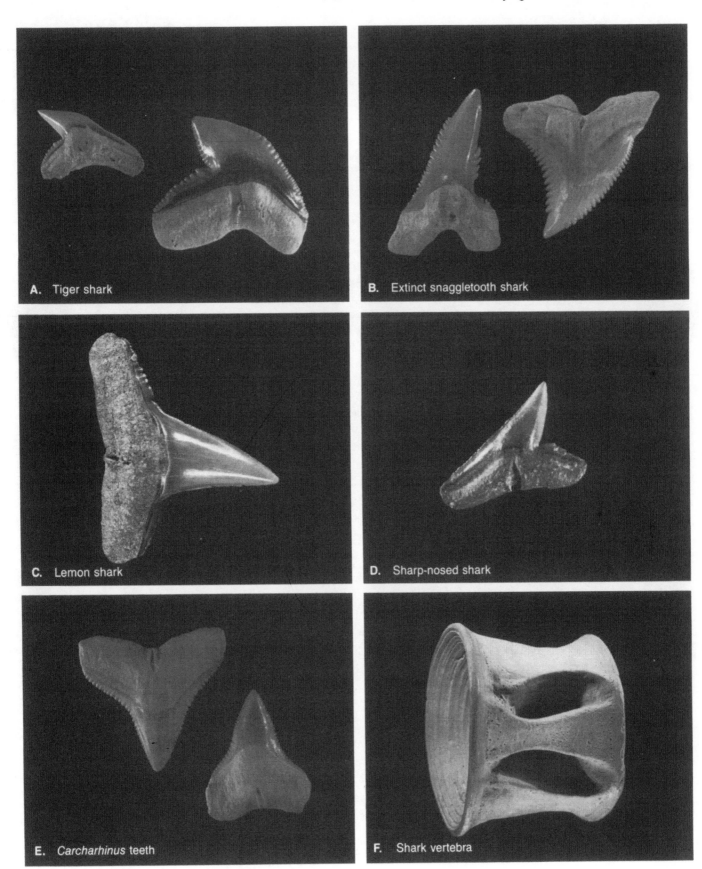

A. Tiger shark

B. Extinct snaggletooth shark

C. Lemon shark

D. Sharp-nosed shark

E. *Carcharhinus* teeth

F. Shark vertebra

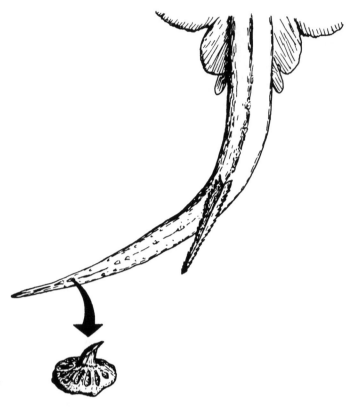

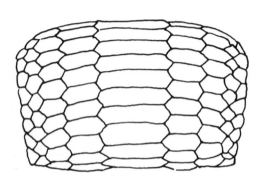

Eagle ray pavement teeth   Dasyatid ray dermal plate and tail spine

PLATE 13

Family Myliobatidae (**eagle rays**)
A. Eagle ray pavement teeth, isolated — largest 1¼ x 1/4 inches (3.2 x .7 cm) Hardee County (FSM)

B. Eagle ray pavement teeth, articulated — 1¾ x 1¾ inches (4.5 x 4.5 cm) Hardee County (FSM)

Family Dasyatidae (**sting rays**)
C. Sting ray tail spine — 5½ x 1 inches (14 x 2.5 cm) and sting ray dermal plates — largest 1⅛ x 3/8 inches (3 x 1 cm) Polk County (FSM)

Class Osteichthyes (the "**bony fish**")

Order Holostei (holostean fish)
Family Lepisosteidae
D. *Lepisosteus* (**garfish**) scales — largest 1⅛ x 3/4 inches (3 x 1.8 cm) Lee County

Order Teleostei (teleost fish)

E. Backbones (vertebrae) of bony fish — largest 1/2 inch (1.5 cm) Lee County

F. Spines and bones of garfish and bony fish — largest 1⅝ inches (4 cm) Lee County

PLATE 13   **Identifying the Fossils You Find**/103

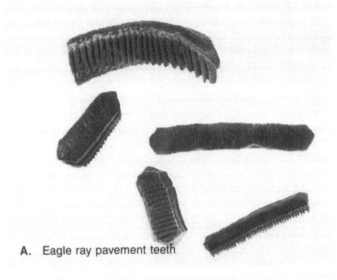

A. Eagle ray pavement teeth

B. Eagle ray pavement teeth, articulated

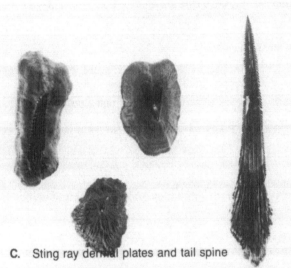

C. Sting ray dermal plates and tail spine

D. Garfish scales

E. Backbones of bony fish

F. Bony fish spines and bones

Diodon mouth part

Barracuda tooth

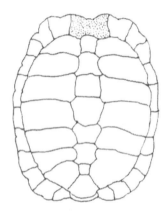

Turtle shell showing scutes. Nuccal scute shaded.

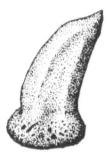

Leg spur of giant land tortoise.

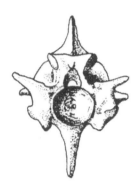
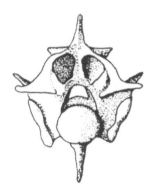

Snake vertebra, rear and front views. Note the ball and socket joint characteristic of reptilian vertebrae.

PLATE 14

Family Sciaenidae (**drum fish**)
A. *Pogonias cromis* — grinding mill and teeth — 2½ x 1½ inches (6.4 x 4 cm) Hillsborough County (FSM)

Family Diodonitidae (**porcupine fish**)
B. *Diodon* mouth part — 1 x 1/2 inch (2.5 x 1.5 cm) Lee County

Family Sphyraenidae (**barracudas**)
C. *Spyraena* tooth — 3/4 x 3/8 inch (2 x 1 cm) Lee County

Class Amphibia (**frogs and salamanders**)

Famiiy Ranidae
D. *Rana* pelvic bone (ilium) of frog — 1⅛ x 1/2 inches (1.2 x .7 cm) Alachua County — Pleistocene (FSM)

Class Reptilia (**reptiles**)

Order Chelonia (**turtles**)
E. Nucchal (see diagram) scutes of representative fossil turtles — largest 5 x 1½ inches (13 x 4 cm) (all FSM)

Two upper right:
Family Trionychidae (**soft shelled turtles**)
Trionyx Union County — Note the "peanut-shell" surface

Two upper left:
Family Emydidae (**pond turtles**)
Pseudemys Alachua County

Three lower right: two scutes and one leg spur:
Family Testudinidae (**tortoises**)
Geochelone — (**land tortoise**) Alachua County

Two lower left:
Family Kinosternidae (**mud turtles**)
Sternothernus Union County

Order Ophidia (**snakes**)
F. Snake vertebrae — largest 1/2 inch (1.5 cm) Lee County — Pleistocene

PLATE 14   **Identifying the Fossils You Find**/105

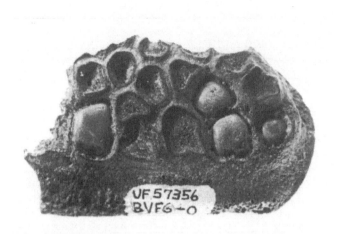

A. Drum fish teeth

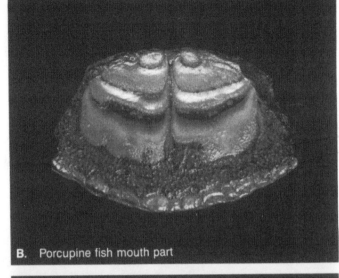

B. Porcupine fish mouth part

C. Barracuda tooth

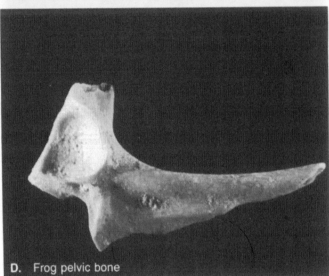

D. Frog pelvic bone

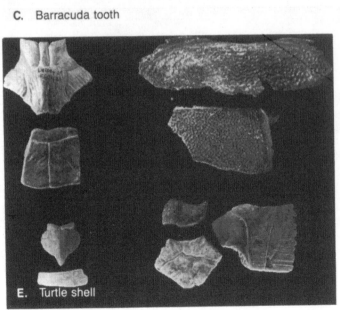

E. Turtle shell

F. Snake vertebrae

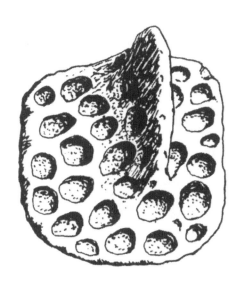

Alligator osteoderm

PLATE 15

Order Crocodilia (**crocodiles and alligators**)

Family Alligatoridae (**alligators**)
A. *Alligator mississippiensis* tooth — 1⅛ x 1/2 inches (3 x 1.1 cm) Columbia County — Pleistocene (FSM)

B. *Alligator mississippiensis* lower jaw (mandible) fragment — 3½ x 1¾ inches (9 x 4.5 cm) Lee County — Pleistocene

C. *Alligator mississippiensis* upper jaw (maxilla) fragment — 5½ x 3½ inches (13 x 9 cm) Columbia County — Pleistocene (FSM)

D. *Alligator mississippiensis* bony armour (osteoderm) — 3 x 2¾ inches (7.5 x 7 cm) Lee County — Pleistocene. Alligator osteoderms are square plates with a central ridge and pitted upper surface.

E. *Alligator mississippiensis* fossilized feces (coprolith) — 3 x 1 inch (8 x 3 cm) Union County — Pleistocene (FSM)

Family Crocodylidae (**crocodiles**)
F. *Gavialosuchus* skull — 33 x 11½ inches (84 x 29 cm) Polk County — Miocene (FSM)

PLATE 15   Identifying the Fossils You Find/107

A. Alligator tooth

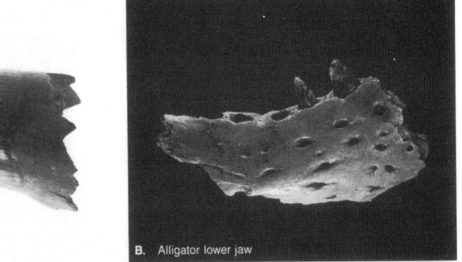

B. *Alligator lower jaw*

C. Alligator upper jaw

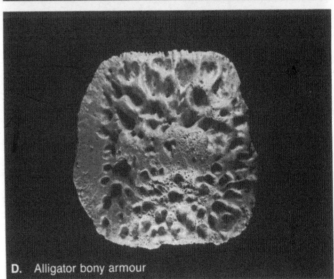

D. Alligator bony armour

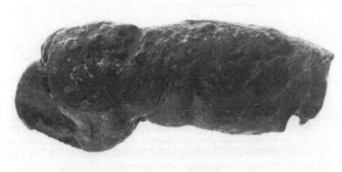

E. Alligator fossilized feces

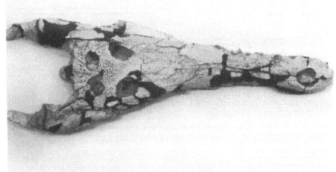

F. *Gavialosuchus* skull

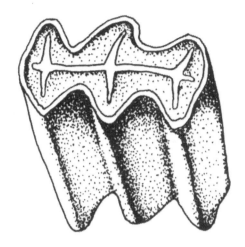

Glyptotherium tooth

PLATE 16

A. *Gavialosuchus* ostoderm — 4⅜ x 3½ inches (11 x 9 cm)   Polk County — Miocene (FSM). *Gavialosuchus* osteoderms are more rounded than *Alligator* and have no central ridge.

Class Aves (**birds**)

Order Pelecaniformes

Family Phalacrocoracidae
B. *Phalacrocorax* (**extinct cormorant**) leg bone (tibiotarsus) — 2⅜ x 1/2 inches (6 x 1.4 cm)   Hardee County — Miocene (FSM)

Class Mammalia (**mammals**)

Order Marsupialia (**marsupials**)

Family Didelphidae
C. *Didelphis virginiana* (**opossum**) mandible — 3⅜ x 1⅝ inches Alachua County — Pleistocene (FSM)

Order Edentata (**edentates**)

D. Bony armour (dermal plates) of edentates

Family Dasypodidae (**armadillos**)

Bottom row — *Dasypus bellus* — largest 1¼ x 3/4 inches (3.2 x 1.8 cm)

Middle row — *Holmesina septentrionalis* — largest 2¾ x 1⅛ inches (7 x 2.8 cm)

Family Glyptodontidae (**glyptodonts**)

Top row — *Glyptotherium* — largest 2 x 2 inches (5 x 5 cm) Hillsborough County — Pleistocene (FSM)

E. *Glyptotherium* dermal plates, articulated — overall 5½ x 2¾ inches (14 x 7 cm)   Hillsborough County — Pleistocene (FSM)

Family Megalonychidae (**ground sloths**)
F. *Megalonyx* teeth — larger 1⅝ x 3/4 inches (4 x 2 cm) Hillsborough County — Pleistocene (FSM)

PLATE 16   **Identifying the Fossils You Find**/109

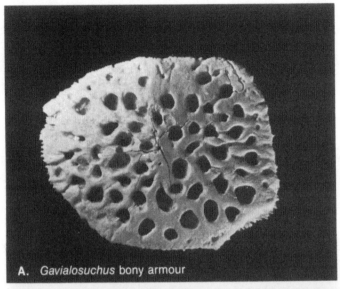

A. *Gavialosuchus* bony armour

B. Extinct cormorant leg bone

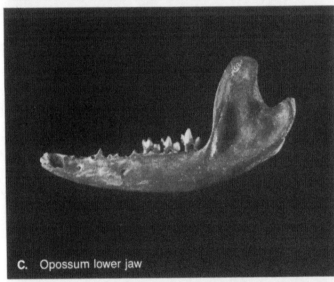

C. Opossum lower jaw

D. Edentate bony armour

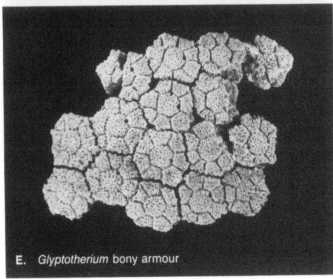

E. *Glyptotherium* bony armour

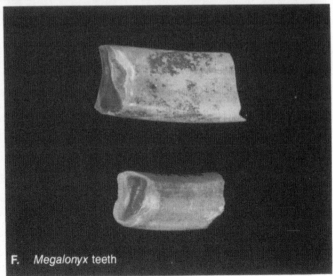

F. *Megalonyx* teeth

PLATE 17

A. *Megalonyx* claw core — 5 x 2 inches (12.5 x 5 cm)
Hillsborough County — Pleistocene (FSM)

Family Megatheriidae (**ground sloths**)
B. *Eremotherium* (**giant ground sloth**) tooth — 5⅛ x 1¾ inches
(13 x 4.5 cm) Alachua County — Pleistocene (FSM). These
large square teeth have no enamel.

Family Mylodontidae (**ground sloths**)
C. *Glossotherium* tooth, crown view (upper) — 1 x 1/2 inch (2.5 x
1.2 cm) and teeth in mandible (lower) — 4¾ x 2½ inches (12 x
6.5 cm) Hillsborough County — Pleistocene (FSM)

Order Chiroptera (**bats**)

Family Desmodontidae (**vampire bats**)
D. *Desmodus rotundus* (**modern vampire bat**) skull — 1 x 9/16
inches (2.5 x 1.5 cm) — courtesy Zoology, FSM. Insert is
extinct Pleistocene vampire bat *Desmodus magnus* maxilla,
same scale, for comparison. Alachua County — Pleistocene
(FSM)

Order Lagomorpha (lagomorphs)

Family Leporidae (**rabbits**)
E. *Sylvilagus* mandible — 2 x 5/8 inches (5 x 1.6 cm) Alachua
County — Pleistocene (FSM)

Order Rodentia (**rodents**)

F. Four rodent mandibles:

Family Cricetidae (**mice**)
Upper left *Sigmodon* (**hispid cotton rat**) Alachua County —
Pleistocene (FSM)

Upper right *Peromyscus* (**cotton mouse**) Alachua County —
Pleistocene (FSM)

Family GEOMYIDAE (**pocket gophers**)
Lower left *Geomys* Alachua County — Pleistocene (FSM)

Family SCIURIDAE (**squirrels**)
Lower right *Glaucomys* (**flying squirrel**) — 1 x ⅜ inches
(2.5 x 1.3 cm) — Pleistocene Citrus County (FSM)

PLATE 17   **Identifying the Fossils You Find**/111

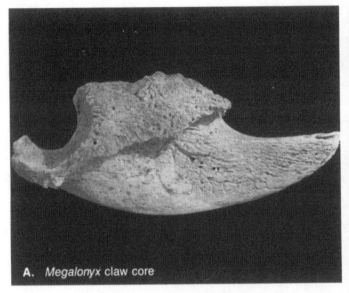

A. *Megalonyx* claw core

B. *Eremotherium* tooth

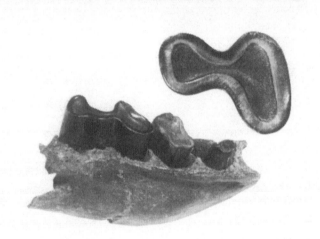

C. *Glossotherium* tooth

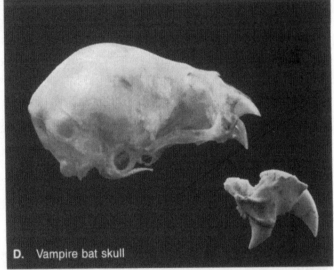

D. Vampire bat skull

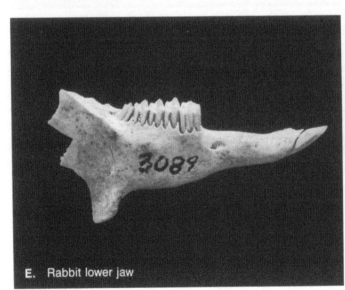

E. Rabbit lower jaw

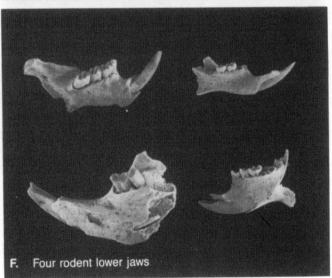

F. Four rodent lower jaws

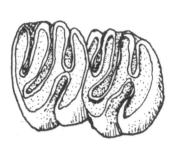
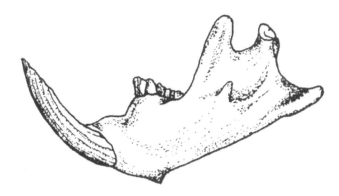

Molar tooth of beaver *Castor* and mandible of giant beaver *Castoroides*

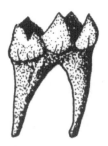

Procyon molar

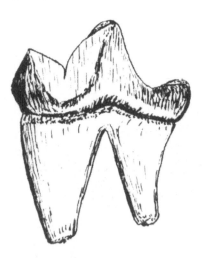

Cheek tooth (carnassial) of dire wolf

PLATE 18

Family Castoridae (**beavers**)
A. *Castor* molar tooth — 1⅛ x 1/2 inches (3 x 1.5 cm) Hillsborough County — Pleistocene (FSM)

Family Hydrochoeridae — (**capybaras**)
B. *Hydrochoerus* molar tooth — 1⅝ x 1⅛ inches (4.2 x 2.8 cm) Suwannee County — Pleistocene (FSM)

Order Carnivora (**carnivores**)

Family Ursidae (**bears**)
C. *Arctodus* (**short-faced bear**) mandible, two canines, and an upper cheek tooth (carnassial) — The mandible measures 9½ x 5 inches (24 x 12.5 cm). Hillsborough County — Pleistocene (FSM)

Family Mustelidae (**weasel family**)
D. *Mephitis* (**skunk**) mandible — 1¾ x 1 inch (4.5 x 2.5 cm) Alachua County — Pleistocene (FSM)

Family Procyonidae (**raccoons**)
E. *Procyon lotor* (**raccoon**) mandible — 3⅛ x 1⅜ inches (8 x 3.5 cm) Levy County — Pleistocene (FSM)

Family Canidae (**dogs, wolves, and coyotes**)
F. *Canis dirus* (**dire wolf**) mandible — 8¼ x 3⅜ inches (21 x 8.5 cm) Hillsborough County — Pleistocene (FSM)

PLATE 18   Identifying the Fossils You Find/113

A. Beaver tooth

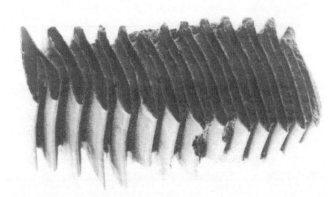

B. Capybara tooth

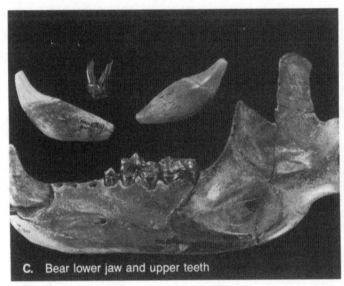

C. Bear lower jaw and upper teeth

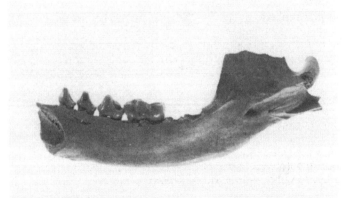

E. Raccoon lower jaw

D. Skunk lower jaw

F. Dire wolf lower jaw

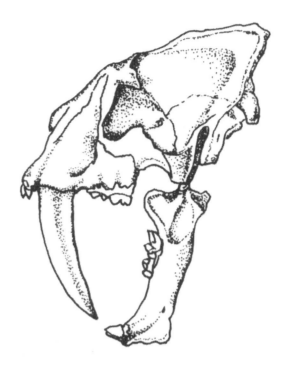

Smilodon skull

PLATE 19

Family Felidae (**cats**)
A. *Smilodon* (**saber-tooth cat**) saber canine tooth and mandible
— saber 6 x 1 inch (15 x 2.5 cm) and jaw 5¼ x 2 inches (13 x
5 cm) Hillsborough County — Pleistocene (FSM)

B. *Felis atrox* (**giant lion**) skull — 16 x 10 inches (41 x 25 cm)
Columbia County — Pleistocene (FSM)

Order Proboscidea (**proboscidians or elephant-like beasts**)

Family Mammutidae (**mastodons**)
C. *Mammut* (**mastodon**) tooth — 7½ x 3½ inches (19 x 9 cm)
Palm Beach County — Pleistocene (FSM). Mastodon teeth
have a relatively simple pattern of cusps compared with
gomphothere teeth (19-F).

D. *Mammut* (**mastodon**) tooth, oblique view — 4¾ x 3⅜ inches
(12 x 8.5 cm) Palm Beach County — Pleistocene (FSM)

E. *Mammut* (**mastodon**) vertebra — 13 x 11 inches (33 x 28 cm)
Dixie County — Pleistocene

Family Gomphotheriidae (**gomphotheres**)
F. *Amebelodon* (**the Florida shovel-tusked gomphothere**) tooth
— 8 x 3½ inches (20 x 9 cm) Alachua County — Miocene
(FSM). There are small cones (conules) between the large
cusps that make gomphothere teeth more complex than
mastodon teeth.

PLATE 19   **Identifying the Fossils You Find**/115

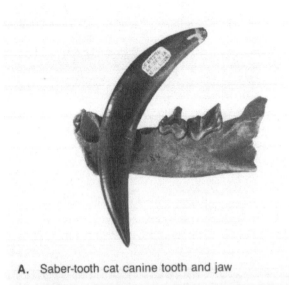

A. Saber-tooth cat canine tooth and jaw

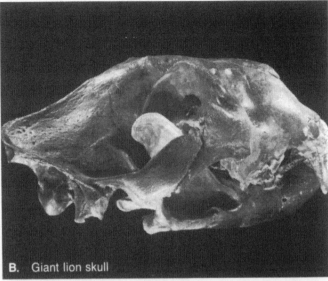

B. Giant lion skull

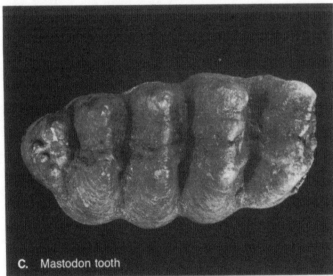

C. Mastodon tooth

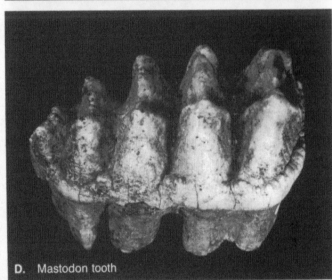

D. Mastodon tooth

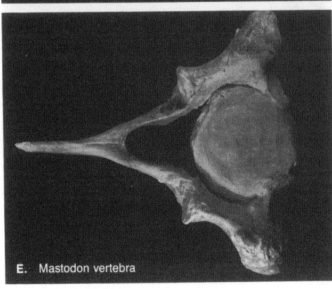

E. Mastodon vertebra

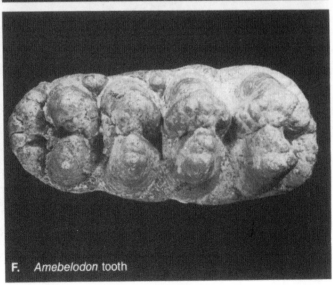

F. *Amebelodon* tooth

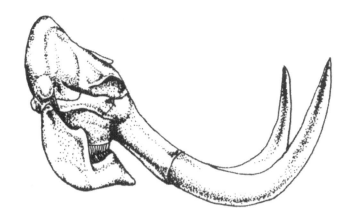

Mammoth skull

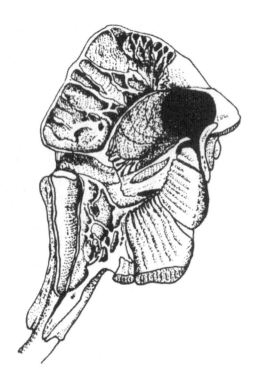

Cross section through an elephant skull showing the air cells and how tooth replacement occurs

PLATE 20

A. *Cuvieronius* (**a Plio-Pleistocene gomphothere**) mandible with teeth — 11¾ x 3⅜ inches (30 x 8.5 cm)   Alachua County — (FSM). As gomphothere teeth wear, complex enamel patterns emerge, often resembling three-leaf clovers (trefoil).

Family Elephantidae (**mammoths and modern elephants**)
B. *Mammuthus meridionalis* (**early Pleistocene mammoth**) tooth — crown view — 10½ x 3 inches (27 x 8 cm)   Hillsborough County (FSM). Early Pleistocene mammoth teeth averaged only 10 to 14 plates.

C. *Mammuthus meridionalis* tooth — same as photograph B, side view — 10½ x 4 inches (27 x 10 cm)

D. *Mammuthus columbi* (**Columbian mammoth**) tooth — 9½ x 10 inches (25 x 24 cm)   Palm Beach County — Pleistocene (FSM). Late Pleistocene mammoth teeth averaged 20 to 30 plates.

E. *Mammuthus* (**mammoth**) skull fragment showing honeycomb-like pattern of air cells — 9 x 4¾ inches (23 x 12 cm) (FSM). The skulls of mammoths contained many air-filled spaces that served to decrease the weight of the head.

F. *Mammuthus* (**mammoth**) tusk fragment — 8½ x 4⅜ inches (22 x 11 cm)   DeSoto County — Pleistocene. Fossil elephant ivory in Florida breaks easily; a plaster jacket is required to recover a tusk intact.

PLATE 20   **Identifying the Fossils You Find**/117

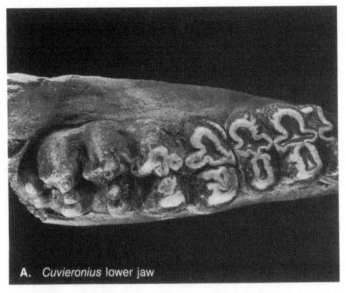

A. *Cuvieronius* lower jaw

B. Mammoth tooth

C. Mammoth tooth

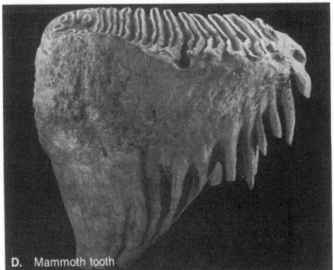

D. Mammoth tooth

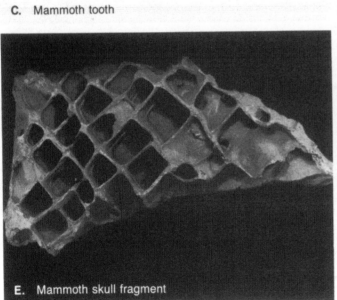

E. Mammoth skull fragment

F. Mammoth tusk fragment

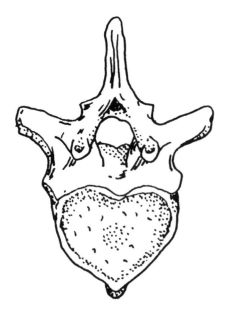
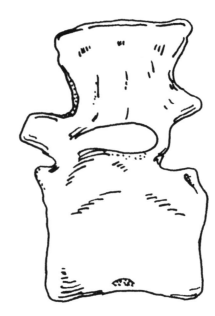

Sea cow vertebra

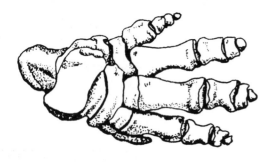

Foot bones of a mammoth

PLATE 21

A. *Mammuthus* (**mammoth**) tusk, cross section — 4⅜ x 4 inches (11 x 10 cm) DeSoto County — Pleistocene Elephant tusk has a characteristic cross-hatched pattern on cross section.

Order Sirenia (**the sea cows — manatees and dugongs**)

Family Dugongidae (**dugongs**)
B. *Metaxytherium* tooth, crown view — 1 x 3/4 inches (2.5 x 2 cm) Hardee County — Miocene (FSM)

C. *Metaxytherium* rib — 7 x 1⅜ inches (18 x 3.5 cm) Polk County — Miocene (FSM). Sea cows have solid bones. Only the vertebral bodies contain sponge-like (cancellous) bone.

Family Trichechidae (**manatees**)
D. *Trichechus* teeth — 1/2 x 1/2 inch (1.5 x 1.5 cm) Gilchrist County — Pleistocene

Order Perissodactyla (**odd-toed hoofed mammals**)

Family Tapiridae (**tapirs**)
E. *Tapirus* upper jaw (maxilla) — 6¾ x 3½ inches (17 x 9 cm) Hillsborough County — Pleistocene (FSM)

F. *Tapirus* molars — largest 1⅝ x 1⅝ inches (4 x 4 cm) Hillsborough County — Pleistocene (FSM)

PLATE 21   **Identifying the Fossils You Find**/119

A. Mammoth tusk, cross section

B. Dugong tooth

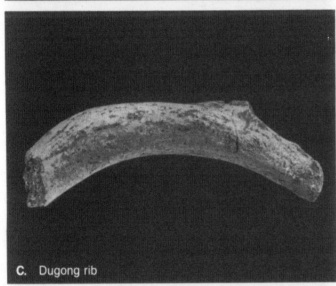

C. Dugong rib

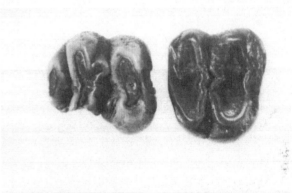

D. Manatee teeth

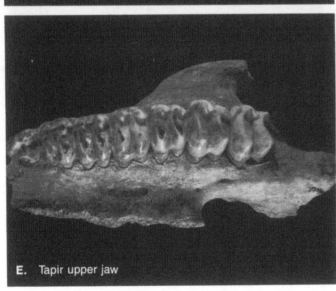

E. Tapir upper jaw

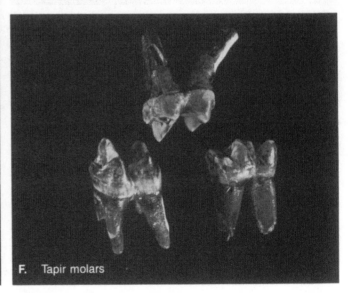

F. Tapir molars

PLATE 22

Family Rhinocerotidae (**rhinoceroses**)
A. *Teleoceras* teeth — 1⅝ x 1⅛ inches (4 x 3 cm) Alachua
County — Miocene (FSM)

B. *Aphelops* mandible — 10 x 2½ inches (26 x 6 cm) Alachua
County — Miocene (FSM)

Family Equidae (**horses**)
C. *Equus* lower jaw (mandible) — 4¾ x 2⅜ inches (12 x 6 cm)
Hillsborough County — Pleistocene (FSM)

D. *Equus* lower molar, three views — 3½ x 1 x 3/4 inches (9 x 2.5
x 1.8 cm) Lee County — Pleistocene

E. *Equus* upper molar, three views — 2½ x 1 x 1 inches (6.5 x 2.5
x 2.5 cm) DeSoto County — Pleistocene

F. *Equus* upper molar — 2 x 1/2 inches (5 x 2.5 cm)
Hillsborough County — Pleistocene (FSM). Horse teeth
develop separated roots as they get older and wear down.

PLATE 22   **Identifying the Fossils You Find** / 121

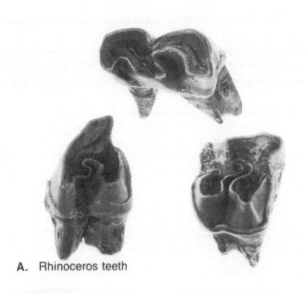

A. Rhinoceros teeth

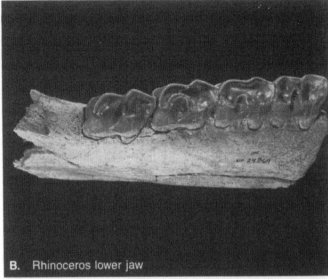

B. Rhinoceros lower jaw

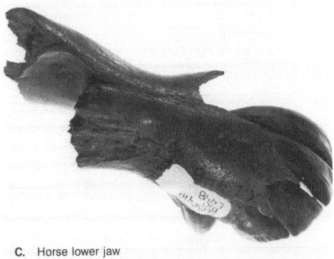

C. Horse lower jaw

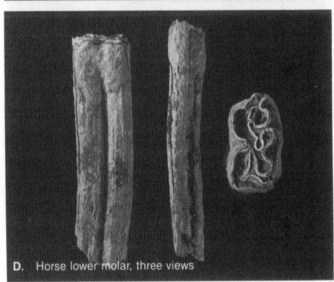

D. Horse lower molar, three views

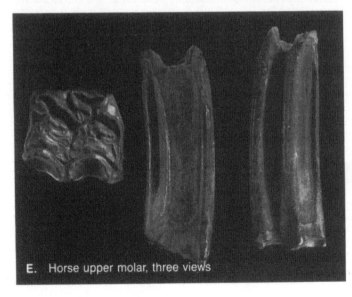

E. Horse upper molar, three views

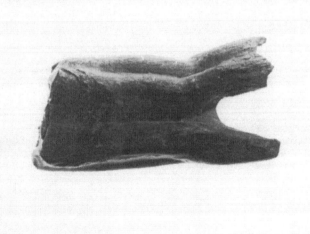

F. Horse upper molar

PLATE 23

A. *Equus* (left) and *Nannippus* (right) upper molars, crown views. The isolated island of enamel (protocone) on the *Nannippus* tooth is characteristic of most three-toed horses.

B. *Equus* ankle bone (astragalus) — 2⅛ x 1¾ inches (5.5 x 4.5 cm) Lee County — Pleistocene

C. *Equus* toe bones with hoof core — overall 7 x 1½ inches (18 x 4 cm) Hillsborough County — Pleistocene (FSM)

Order Artiodactyla (**even-toed hoofed mammals**)

Family Tayassuidae (**peccaries**)
D. *Platygonus* mandible — 8¼ x 5⅛ inches (21 x 13 cm) Alachua County — Pleistocene (FSM)

E. *Platygonus* mandible fragment — 2 x 1/2 inches (5 x 1.3 cm) Hillsborough County — Pleistocene (FSM)

F. *Mylohyus* mandible — 10¼ x 4 inches (26 x 10 cm) Hillsborough County — Pleistocene (FSM)

PLATE 23   **Identifying the Fossils You Find** / 123

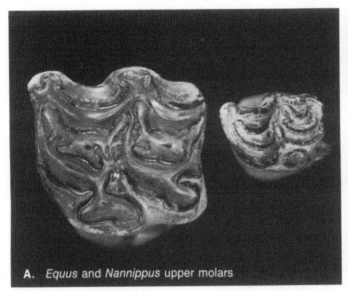

A. *Equus* and *Nannippus* upper molars

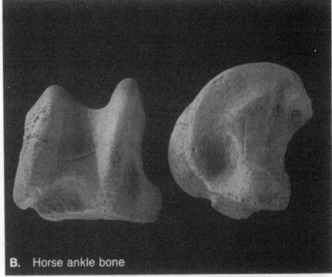

B. Horse ankle bone

C. Horse toe bones and hoof core

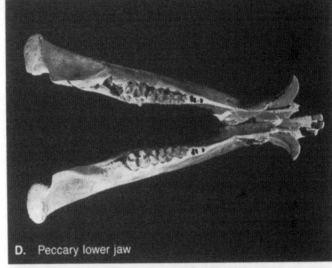

D. Peccary lower jaw

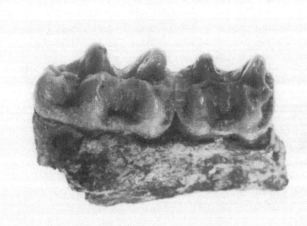

E. Peccary lower jaw fragment

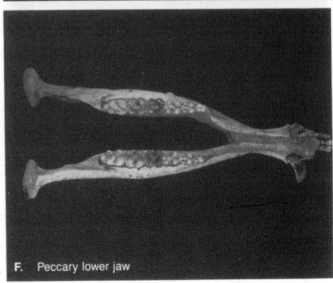

F. Peccary lower jaw

PLATE 24

A. *Mylohyus* mandible fragment — 2⅜ x 1 inches (6 x 2.5 cm) Hillsborough County — Pleistocene (FSM)

Family Camelidae (**camel-like and llama-like beasts**)
B. *Hemiauchenia* maxilla and molar teeth — the maxilla measures 4¾ x 2⅜ inches (12 x 6 cm) Hillsborough County — Pleistocene (FSM). *Hemiauchenia* had finely ridged (crenelated) teeth and was a larger animal than *Paleolama*.

C. *Paleolama* maxilla (upper) — 4¾ x 2⅜ inches (12 x 6 cm) and mandible (lower) — 4¾ x 2 inches (12 x 5 cm) Hillsborough County — Pleistocene (FSM)

D. *Paleolama* or *Hemiauchenia* neck bone (cervical vertebra) — 6 x 2⅜ inches (16 x 6 cm) Hillsborough County — Pleistocene (FSM). This elongate neck vertebra is characteristic of both genera of Pleistocene camelids.

E. *Paleolama* or *Hemiauchinia* cannon bone (fused 2nd and 3rd metatarsal bones) — 4⅜ x 2⅜ inches (11 x 6 cm) Hillsborough County — Pleistocene (FSM). The partially split cannon bone is found in camelids, bison, and deer.

F. *Paleolama* or *Hemiauchenia* ankle bone (astragalus) — 2½ x 2 inches (6.5 x 5 cm) Lee County — Pleistocene. Compare this ankle bone with the obliquely grooved astragalus of the horse.

PLATE 24   Identifying the Fossils You Find/125

A. Peccary lower jaw fragment

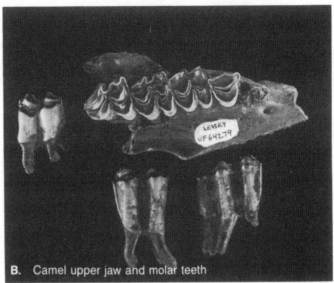

B. Camel upper jaw and molar teeth

C. Camel upper and lower jaw

D. Camel neck bone

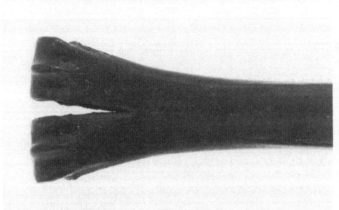

E. Camel cannon bone

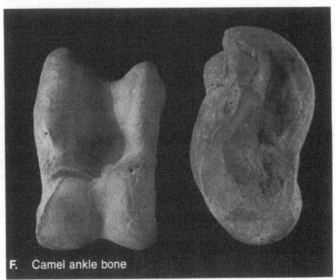

F. Camel ankle bone

Mandible of archaeocete whale

PLATE 25

Family Cervidae (**deer**)
A. *Odocoileus* mandible and antler — The antler measures 9 x
1¾ inches (23 x 4.5 cm) Columbia County — Pleistocene
(FSM)

Family Antilocapridae (**pronghorns**)
B. *Capromeryx* (**antelope**) mandible — 3 x 1 inches (7.5 x 2.5
cm) Levy County — Pleistocene (FSM)

C. *Capromeryx* (**antelope**) mandible fragment — 1⅜ x 1⅛ inches
(3.5 x 3 cm) Levy County — Pleistocene (FSM)

Family Bovidae (**cow, goats, sheep, and bison**)
D. *Bison antiquus* maxilla (upper) and mandible (lower) — both
6¼ x 1⅛ inches (16 x 3 cm) Columbia County — Pleistocene
(FSM)

Order Cetacea (**whales**)

Suborder Archaeoceti (**extinct zeuglodont whales**)

E. *Dorudon serratus* teeth — larger 3¼ x 2½ inches (8.5 x 6.5
cm) Alabama — Eocene (FSM)

Suborder Odontoceti (**toothed whales and dolphins**)

F. Sperm whale tooth — 4 x 1¼ inches (10 x 3.3 cm) Lee
County — Pliocene

PLATE 25   **Identifying the Fossils You Find**/127

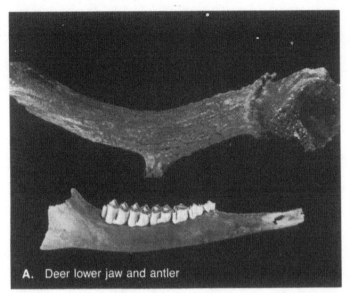

A. Deer lower jaw and antler

B. Antelope lower jaw

C. Antelope lower jaw fragment

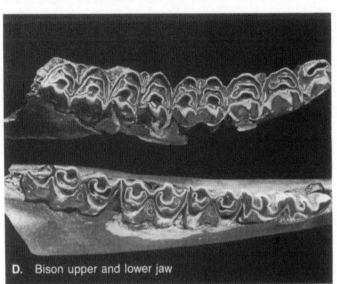

D. Bison upper and lower jaw

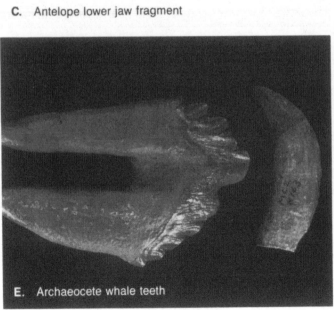

E. Archaeocete whale teeth

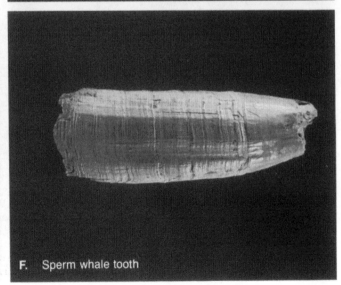

F. Sperm whale tooth

PLATE 26

A. Sperm whale tooth — 4⅜ x 1⅜ inches (11 x 3.5 cm) DeSoto County — Plio-Pleistocene (Courtesy Joe Latvis)

B. *Pomatodelphis* (**dolphin**) maxilla fragment — 4¾ x 7/8 inches (12 x 2.2 cm) Polk County — Miocene-Pliocene (FSM)

C. Dolphin tooth — 3/4 x 1/4 inch (2 x .6 cm) Lee County — Pliocene

Suborder Mysticeti (**baleen or whalebone whales**)

Family Balaenopteridae
D. *Balaenoptera* inner ear bone (auditory bulla) — 4 x 2¾ inches (10 x 7 cm) Lee County — Pliocene (FSM)

E. *Balaenoptera* neck bone (cervical vertebra) — 10 x 4¾ inches (25 x 11 cm) Hillsborough County — Pliocene (FSM)

PLATE 26   **Identifying the Fossils You Find**/129

A. Sperm whale tooth

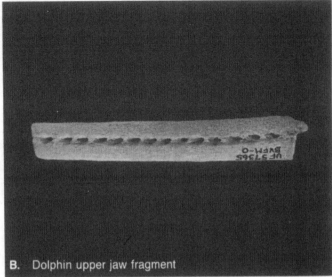

B. Dolphin upper jaw fragment

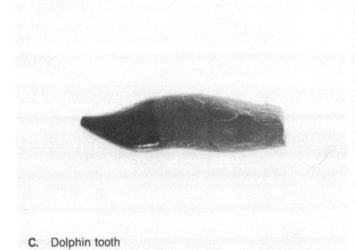

C. Dolphin tooth

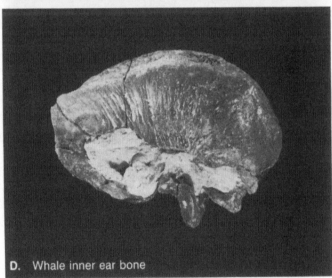

D. Whale inner ear bone

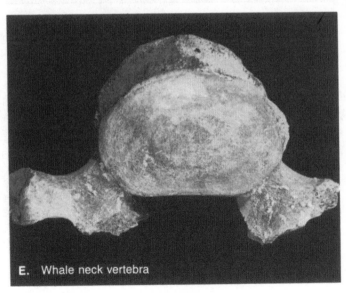

E. Whale neck vertebra

Sinkholes trapped animals throughout Florida's history.

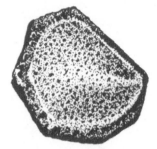

Holmesina septentrionalis dermal plate

CHAPTER 6

How Fossils Were Formed

Many areas of North America where prehistoric animal life must have been abundant have no surviving record of the beasts that lived there. Clearly, for Florida to have such a wealth of fossils, some special conditions had to be present.

It is a general rule that to become preserved well enough to last thousands or millions of years, an animal must have hard parts and must be buried soon after death in some sort of material that prevents disturbance and keeps out oxygen and agents of decay.

Although the bones of vertebrates qualify as hard parts, they don't commonly fossilize, particularly if the animal dies on land. Ordinarily, bones are scattered and eaten by other animals. Those left exposed in dry situations weather and crumble. In wet areas, they are destroyed by plant roots, soil acids, and bacteria. Some wash into swiftly moving streams where they are worn and broken.

In Florida, however, a variety of features greatly increased the chances of animal bones being preserved.

Florida appears to have been geologically tranquil during the past 25 to 30 million years. No earthquakes dropped pieces of the state into the ocean, no volcanoes buried the land beneath ash or lava, and no mountains pushed up to alter rainfall patterns and create rushing waters. The flat terrain had few turbulent rivers to scatter and destroy bones. Abundant rainfall washed animal carcasses or bones into ponds or slowly moving streams where sand, clay, or muck soon covered them, sealing out oxygen and preventing bacterial decomposition. This wet environment also preserved wood, leaves, and pollen that offer information about the climate and surroundings where ancient animals lived. More swiftly moving rivers carried animal remains into estuaries. There the bones settled, often to be concentrated and covered by the action of tides and storms.

Since the early Miocene, warm climate and a mixture of grasslands and woods favored a great diversity and abundance of land animals. The sheer number of animals that lived in Florida over the past 25 million years greatly increased the material available for fossilization.

Limestone that lies beneath so much of the state assisted fossilization in a unique way. Groundwater picked up carbon dioxide and weak organic acids from decaying leaves and slowly dissolved the limestone. Over millions of years, the water left solution holes in the form of caves and underground streams within the stone, producing a geologic landscape called **karst**.

The ground water in turn became alkaline, charged with calcium carbonate from the limestone. Throughout

Florida's past, ground water levels rose and fell in response to sea level changes. When water levels dropped, the caves and underground streams emptied, losing the support that the water furnished. The thin crust separating these caverns from the surface collapsed, producing limestone sinkholes ideally suited for trapping animals. Creatures fell into these sinks and died. Scavengers came to feed on the victims and were themselves trapped. Bats inhabited some sinks and others were home to owls.

The owls added more than their own remains: the bones of small animals that the owls ate — mice, moles, and shrews — were regurgitated by these birds as pellets. Owl pellets provide a fine source of tiny vertebrates otherwise rarely fossilized.

Many sinkholes eventually became ponds that added fish, turtles, and frogs to the bone pile. Thus the layers built up, with sand and clay periodically washed in to cover the animal remains.

Certain hard parts of animals that are made of protein, such as hooves and the outer layers of some horns, don't fossilize. Rhinoceros horn is all protein; so is the flexible "whalebone" strainer in the mouths of baleen whales. Neither survives in Florida as a fossil. On the other hand, the bony cores of hooves and horns are preserved well.

Much of the state that is high and dry today was once covered by the sea. Bones of whales and dolphins were fossilized when sand and mud covered them on the bottom of shallow bays and estuaries. Shark teeth, produced in huge numbers, were preserved with only a change in color. They are the commonest vertebrate fossil in Florida. The remains of mollusks and echinoids made of a type of calcium carbonate called calcite were quite durable and are often found today. Shells made of a less chemically stable form of calcium carbonate called aragonite, were sometimes dissolved. In formations like the Ocala Limestone and Tamiami Formation, traces of aragonitic shells and corals remain only as external molds (outside impressions) or internal molds (inside impressions); the shell itself has completely disappeared.

Dense concentrations of sea bottom life, such as the Pinecrest and Caloosahatchee beds, have layers that were fossilized over a very short period of time. Shells, crabs, corals, and barnacles seem to have been suddenly covered, leaving them in lifelike positions and nearly perfect condition. The storm surge of a great hurricane may well account for this mass burial.

The Stages of Sinkhole Formation

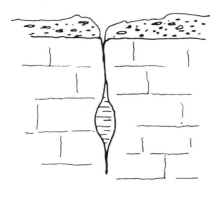

1. A fissure in limestone fills with groundwater.

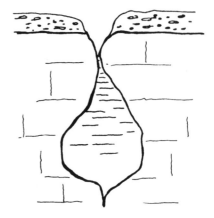

2. A water-filled cave forms.

5. The roof collapses. Owls inhabit the cave.

6. The sheer sides of the sinkhole make it a natural trap for large animals.

3. The water level falls.

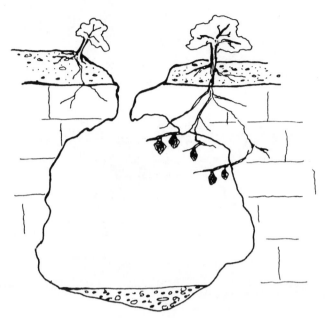

4. The cave becomes a home
for bats.

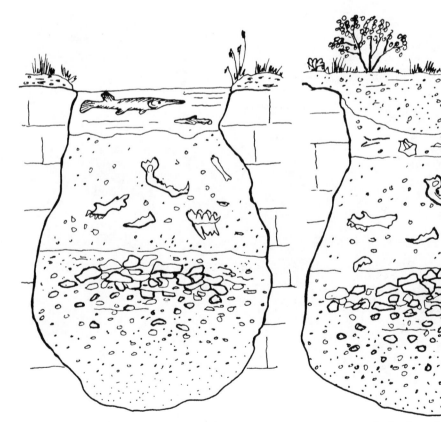

7. The partially filled sinkhole
becomes a pond.

8. In time, the sinkhole is
completely filled.

MOBLEY

Giant Pleistocene lion stalking two camelids.

Whale teeth

CHAPTER 7

Florida's Fossil History

Life began on the planet Earth over 3.8 billion years ago and the fossil record traces the continuous development of living things during this vast period of time.

Florida has been a part of the North American continent for 200 million years, but it was under water most of that time. The ancient rocks are buried deeply and fossils can be readily found only from the past 50 million years. But this 50-million-year history encompasses a fascinating time in earth history, the height of the Age of Mammals.

The chart on the facing page is the Geologic Time Scale of the Cenozoic — the Era in which Florida's known past is contained.

The Early Cenozoic

The event that marked the end of the Cretaceous Era, some 65 million years ago, is thought to be the result of a meteor strike near present-day Mexico. It is thought to be the second-worst extinction event in the history of the earth, wiping out as many as 80 percent of all species. Reptiles, rulers of the earth for the preceding 150 million years, mostly went extinct. Dinosaurs disappeared along with a lot of other life forms—both sea and land dwellers. As the earth recovered from this sweeping destruction, animal life took a new evolutionary turn.

The fossil record shows that mammals began to multiply, to diversify into many new species, and to spread into many new ecological niches. In this process, they developed an incredible variety of sizes, shapes, diets, ways of getting around, and methods of offense and defense. Mammals got bigger, smarter, fiercer, and faster. An increase in oxygen in the world's atmosphere that began in the Cenozoic may have contributed to mammalian success: more oxygen enabled the increased metabolic rate, characteristic of mammals, to occur. Some invaded the sea and others learned to fly. Dinosaurs had begun the transition into birds in the Cretaceous, and in the Cenozoic a wonderful proliferation of birds took place.

The Cenozoic of Florida

Million Years Ago	Epoch	Invertebrates	Sharks	Mammals
	RECENT			
0.1	PLEISTOCENE	Chione cancellata	Carcharodon carcharias	Smilodon / Bison
1.8	PLIOCENE	Arca wagneriana	Isurus hastalis	Equus / Glyptotherium
5	MIOCENE	Ecphora quadricostata / Nodipecten condylomatus	Hemipristis serra	Teleoceras / Amebelodon
24.5	OLIGOCENE	Rhyncholampas gouldii	Galeocerdo aduncas	Mesohippus
37.5	EOCENE	Foraminifera / Eupatagus antillarum	Carcharodon auriculatus	Basilosaurus

Archaeocete whale tooth.

The Eocene

Florida's earliest epoch that can be collected today, the Eocene, began 54 million years ago and lasted 16.5 million years.

The earliest part of the Cenozoic Era, the Paleocene, left no surface record in Florida. In fact, Florida probably didn't emerge from the sea until the Cenozoic was half over. But during the Eocene, about 50 million years ago, in the open Gulf of Mexico, one-celled organisms named foraminifera began to form a limestone that was to become the backbone of the Florida peninsula. The fragile skeletons (tests) of these marine creatures settled to the bottom in countless billions and, together with shells, corals, and other shallow water marine organisms, compacted into a calcium carbonate stone. Also on this sea bottom lived a myriad of sand dollars and sea urchins — some 30 species of echinoids that fossilized along with the foraminifera. Sharks — *Carcharadon auriculatus*, *Otodus obliquus*, and *Odontaspis microta* — inhabited these waters and left their teeth to become fossils. Archaeocete whales, snake-like and primitive, swam in this sea and one genus, *Basilosaurus*, grew to be 65 feet long. Its serrated teeth also became part of the fossil record.

Other inhabitants were primitive sea cows that were relatives of manatees, sea turtles, and eight-foot-long (paleophid) marine snakes, related to boas.

Today this Eocene marine deposit, called the Ocala Limestone, is found close to the surface in North and North-central Florida and in the panhandle. It includes several subdivisions, the Inglis, Williston, and Crystal River formations. The cream-colored Ocala Limestone, 99 percent pure calcium carbonate, contains the fossils of countless foraminifera, some the size and shape of a quarter, called "coin fossils," plus many beautiful echinoids, pectens, coiled nautiloids, occasional shark teeth, and the rare traces of archaeocete whales.

Rhyncholampas gouldii

The Oligocene

The Oligocene epoch began 37.5 million years ago and lasted 13 million years.

At the end of the Eocene, some 37 million years ago, a major change in the world's climate occurred. From causes still unclear, ocean temperatures fell a few degrees and many of the echinoids that had flourished in the Eocene became extinct. Sea level slowly fell, and toward the end of the Oligocene, the shallow limestone layers that had formed during the preceding 20 or 30 million years began to emerge from the waters of the Gulf of Mexico. Foraminifera and other sea bottom creatures began building a new kind of limestone in the surrounding shallow waters, but only one sea urchin, *Rhyncholampas gouldii* was abundant.

A new group of sharks left their teeth behind to fossilize: *Negaprion brevirostris, Hemipristis serra, Rhizoprionodon terrae-novae,* and *Galeocerdo aduncas.* But sea cows were rare and whales were totally absent. This Oligocene marine deposit is called the Suwannee Limestone and today is exposed in quarries in Suwannee, Pasco, and Hernando counties and along the Suwannee River in Columbia County. In the panhandle the Oligocene is represented by the porous, white, Marianna Limestone of Jackson County.

Oligocene Florida probably started out as a cluster of islands before it grew into a peninsula. Gaps between the islands were slowly bridged by soil washed down from the continental land mass and sand and shell fragments deposited by ocean currents. From time to time the sea rose and further washed and eroded the land, only to fall again to an even lower level.

By the time Florida began to offer a home to land animals, a lot of mammalian and avian evolution had taken place elsewhere in the world. It was a remarkable assortment of animals that moved down from the North American continent into the newly drained land that was

Florida. A single 28-million-year-old site in Alachua County yields the earliest record of Oligocene land animals in Florida. Among them were *Mesohippus*, a small three-toed horse, numerous unusual rodents, turtles, snakes, and several oreodonts — New World grass-eaters that probably looked like pigs.

Fossils of Oligocene terrestrial animals are very rare in Florida and they give us only a glimpse of the profusion of life that was to come in the next epoch — the Miocene.

Rhinoceros tooth

The Miocene

The Miocene Epoch began 24.5 million years ago and lasted 19.5 million years, ending 5 million years ago. It is the longest epoch in the Cenozoic Era. Though a late-starter as a home for land animals, Florida in the Miocene was a bountiful host.

Sea level continued generally downward, exposing more and more land. Florida was distinctly tropical; temperatures were 9 to 12 degrees Fahrenheit (3 to 4 degrees Centigrade) warmer than today. But the glacial cycles that were to result in world climate changes, right up to the present time, first occurred in the Miocene.

Despite advances in understanding the Earth's weather, glacial cycles, or ice ages, remain puzzling global events. Our climate today represents the tail end of the most recent (Wisconsin) glaciation. From causes not fully understood, polar ice begins to build up, signaling the onset of a glacial period. As the ice mass grows, the world supply of water is increasingly trapped in glaciers and sea level falls. Land area increases, rainfall diminishes, and the earth grows colder. Finally, the process is reversed and the polar ice starts to melt. Seas rise and temperatures again become moderate.

One such global rise in sea level took place in the middle Miocene, about 13 million years ago. Toward the close of the Miocene, some 5 or 6 million years ago, the sea fell briefly almost to present-day levels. This sea level drop appears to have resulted from a major buildup of ice over Antarctica rather than northern hemisphere glaciation.

The Florida shoreline in the late Miocene.

Rainfall was abundant during much of the Miocene and there were probably distinct wet and dry seasons. The climate became cooler and drier as the epoch progressed, but Florida was spared the extremes of drought and cold that were to affect much of the world.

A land bridge across the Bering Strait permitted migration of land animals between North America and Eurasia during most of the Miocene. As the climate became colder, use of this bridge was increasingly restricted to cold-tolerant animals.

No connection between North and South America existed until late Miocene. Even this initial link between the two continents was probably a line of islands separated by sizable water gaps. A complete land bridge between North and South America was in place by the end of the Pliocene. But the late Miocene saw the earliest mixing of animals between two great land masses that had been separate for 50 million years.

And so animals moved into Florida, first migrating southward and eastward from continental North America where life was already abundant.

Miocene Florida offered a multitude of habitats and foods, and living conditions were suitable for an enormous variety of animals. Forested areas alternated with grassy plains, and grasslands probably became more extensive as the epoch progressed. Myriads of slow-moving rivers and streams carried off the tropical rainfall. Much of the coast was estuary and shallow bay. Low wetlands and marsh fringed the watercourses with succulent vegetation. Groundwater picked up carbon dioxide and organic acids from decaying vegetation and trickled into the peninsula's limestone foundation, gradually dissolving it and forming underground caverns and rivers. Occasional caverns opened to the surface and began trapping animals, a process that was to continue for 20 million years.

During the first half of the Miocene, living things increased in kind and number, spreading and adapting to every available habitat. During the second half of the era, as conditions became cooler and drier, the variety and abundance of some animals declined. But Florida's fauna never grew sparse. The late Miocene saw carnivores reaching Florida from Eurasia and sloths arriving from South America.

Life in the surrounding seas was equally prolific. Marine deposits trace the changing shoreline as the ocean rose and fell. During the first ten million years or so of the Miocene, a sandy limestone was deposited from the panhandle to Central Florida in shallow seas, brackish bays, and estuaries. It is today given several names, one of which is the Tampa Limestone; its fossil mollusks survive mostly as molds. In middle Miocene times, a layer of sand, clay, and silt, with occasional areas of limestone, was formed in warm coastal environments. It extended from North Florida and the mid panhandle down to South-Central Florida. Over most of its extent, this deposit is called the Hawthorn Formation. Some of the finest examples of mid-Miocene mollusks are beautifully preserved in a 12-million-year-old shell marl called the Chipola Formation which is exposed in Calhoun, Washington, and Jackson counties in the panhandle. A good marker of mid to late Miocene marine layers is the gastropod *Ecphora quadricostata* (shown in Chapter 5).

During the last eight to ten million years of the Miocene, there were several formations that built up in the warm waters skirting the Gulf coast of Florida. In the panhandle, late Miocene shells and corals that are today called the Jackson Bluff Formation, crop out along the Oclocknee River banks in Leon, Gadsden, and Liberty counties. In Central Florida, the Bone Valley Formation was laid down along bays and in the mouths of rivers when the bones of Miocene fish and marine mammals were buried in silt and clay that washed from the land. When sea level dropped, land animals covered the exposed coastal plain and their remains added a terrestrial layer to the fossil record. Later with another sea level rise, the cycle was repeated. This wonderful melange of land and sea creatures spans some 10 to 15 million years. Today, these fossils are exposed by extensive open-pit phosphate mining operations in Hillsborough, Hardee, Manatee, and De Soto counties. Earliest Bone Valley layers overlie the Hawthorn Formation and contain dolphins, bony fish, sharks, rays, and sea cows. Later marine layers contain sea turtles and younger marine mammals such as porpoises and baleen whales.

In latest Miocene times, a rich shell bed known as the Tamiami Formation was laid down in quiet bays and estuaries from Central to South Florida. Tamiami fossils include huge barnacles, varied corals, and a multitude of mollusks. Today, the mollusks and corals are largely gone, leaving only intricate internal and external molds. But the oysters, scallops, and giant barnacles survive intact.

Marine mammals changed greatly in the Miocene. The archaeocete whales had long been extinct and the long-beaked dolphins, abundant in the early Miocene, became rare by the close of the epoch. Several toothed whales and at least three types of baleen whales appeared in the seas around Florida. Sea cows of the genus *Metaxytherium* were abundant in coastal waters and their fossils are common in Bone Valley deposits.

Several sharks common in Florida's Miocene waters subsequently became extinct. These include the large mako *Isurus hastalis,* the giant *Carcharadon megalodon,* the snaggletoothed *Hemipristis serra,* and a sand shark, *Odontaspis cuspidata.*

Land animals in Florida reached their climax in the Miocene, and Florida's fossil record is the finest in eastern North America. Three important Miocene fossil sites illustrate how the bones and teeth of these diverse animals came to be concentrated and preserved.

The **Thomas Farm Site** in Gilchrist County is a bone bed from the early Miocene, about 18 million years ago. The actual deposit measures a few hundred feet in diameter, but fossils are incredibly abundant. It represents a sinkhole that trapped animals over a short period of time, geologically speaking. Each rainy season washed in sand and clay to preserve the bones.

The **Love Site** in Alachua County is about nine million years old. It typifies swamp and stream deposits. Animals living in a marsh environment, and other animals that came to these wet areas to drink, left their remains in great abundance. Bones were periodically flushed into a stream where they collected in deep holes on the stream bottom and were subsequently covered with sediments. One of these fossil-filled pockets, formed by a bend in the ancient stream, has furnished over 100 species of vertebrates.

The **Bone Valley** deposits in Central Florida include terrestrial faunas that span the middle Miocene to early Pliocene (from 15 million to 4 million years ago). They probably represent animals whose carcasses and bones washed into rivers and were carried down to bays where bones accumulated in great quantity and were subsequently sorted and covered by tidal action.

The land animals that flourished in Miocene Florida are too numerous to describe in detail, but the following examples suggest something of their wonderful diversity.

Reptiles included the giant land tortoise, *Geochelone,* whose shell sometimes reached six feet in length. There were iguanas, gila monsters, and the narrow-snouted, fast-swimming crocodile *Gavialosuchus,* that grew to 20 feet in length. Alligators were plentiful and they looked much like they do today. There were lots of turtles, and among the many snakes were two kinds of vipers and the coral snake *Micrurus.*

Birds became more numerous and diverse, occupying many habitats during the epoch. There were perching, shore, wading, and sea birds. Among them were varieties of cormorant, anhinga, osprey, ibis, flamingo, vulture, kite, turkey, and hawk.

Thomas Farm, an early Miocene site in Gilchrist County.

Excavating at Love Site in Alachua County. (FSM)

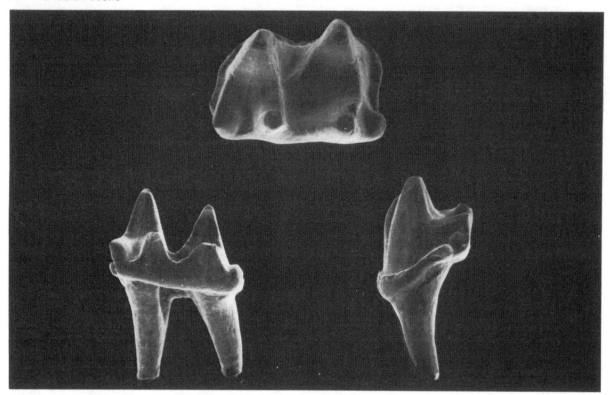

Scanning electron micrograph of the tooth of the insect-eating Miocene bat *Suaptenos whitii* from Thomas Farm. The actual tooth measures only 1.3 millimeters in length. (Courtesy FSM)

The earliest Miocene mammals were confined to the northern part of Florida since the lower part of the peninsula had not yet emerged from the sea. But fossils of late Miocene land animals have been found as far south as Sarasota and De Soto counties.

Among the rodents, squirrels (which are ancient mammals traceable back to the Eocene) were present in Florida throughout the Miocene. Rat and mouse-like animals called cricetid rodents appeared late in the Miocene.

Several genera of bats were present from early Miocene times. Probably many more were around, but bat teeth are of pinhead size and, unfortunately, easily overlooked in fossil deposits.

Sloths (edentates) arrived in the late Miocene, probably migrating along the island chain that formed the first link between North and South America. Two primitive forms, *Pliometanastes* and *Thinobadistes*, were the ancestors of sloths that were to become common in the Pleistocene.

Carnivores included several early Miocene dog-like beasts. *Daphoenodon* and *Amphicyon* were large "bear dogs" and *Tomarctus* was a primitive bone-crushing dog. The middle Miocene hyenoid dog *Aleurodon* was a predator-scavenger, as was the late Miocene *Osteoborus*.

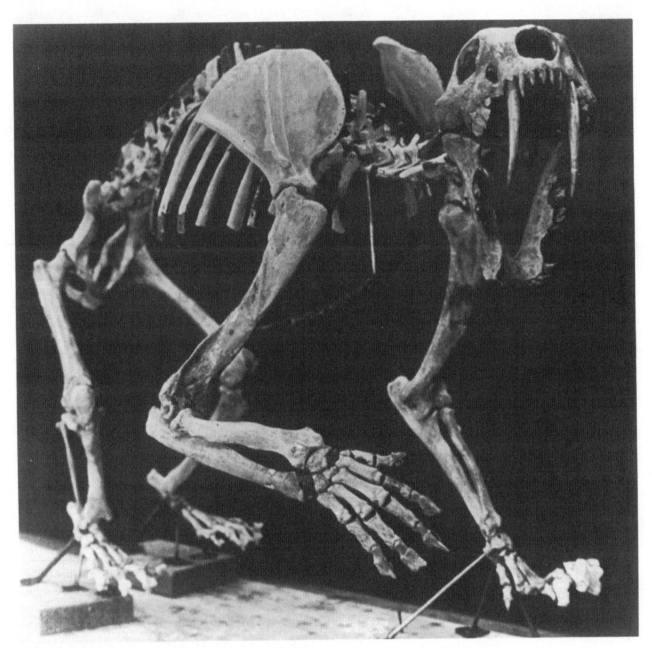

Barbourofelis skeleton from Love Site. (Courtesy FSM)

One of the earliest members of the bear family (ursids) was the large *Hemicyon* from the early Miocene.

Cat-like carnivores appeared in the middle Miocene. *Barbourofelis*, a carnivore weighing up to 120 pounds, had upper canines modified into long narrow blades. Referred to as false sabercat, *Barbourofelis* is found more abundantly at the nine-million-year-old Love Site than anywhere else in the world, and the only complete skeleton of this animal has been prepared from Florida fossil material.

Another large cat-like predator of the same age, *Nimravides*, was about 20 percent heavier than *Barbourofelis* and similar in proportion to a jaguar, with upper canines that were enlarged but circular in cross section rather than saber-like. *Nimravides* was a member of the felids or true cats. Two true sabercats, the large *Machairodus* and the small *Megantereon*, originated in Eurasia and arrived in Florida in latest Miocene times. *Megantereon* was probably the ancestor of the huge Pleistocene sabercat *Smilodon*.

Miocene elephant-beasts (proboscidians) migrated into North America from Eurasia and entered Florida about 15 million years ago. They consisted mostly of gomphotheres which had trunks like elephants but had both upper and lower tusks. *Gomphotherium* had rather straight tusks which were round in cross section. Other gomphotheres such as *Amebelodon* had an elongated "chin," lower tusks that were widened like shovels, and large upper tusks that wore against the shovel-like lower incisors. *Rhynchotherium* had sharply down-turned lower tusks and jaw. These features may have enabled gomphotheres to scoop and devour succulent water plants. All had very similar massive teeth with rounded cusps and many accessory little cones (conules) between the larger cusps.

Rhinoceroses were found in Florida through most of the Miocene. An early Miocene rhino was the large hornless *Floridoceras*. Of similar age was the medium-sized *Menoceras* which had a nasal horn. A late Miocene rhinoceros, the horned *Teleoceras*, had a long, heavily built body and short stout legs, and probably spent much of its life immersed in water like today's hippopotamus. *Aphelops*, from the same period, was hornless and had relatively long legs. Rhinos disappeared from Florida at the end of the Miocene.

North America was the evolutionary cradle of horses and the Miocene was a time of horse proliferation and change. In the early Miocene, horses were small, three-toed, browsing animals that lived in forest environments. As the epoch progressed, they developed into large,

Drawings of Miocene rhinoceroses. Above: *Teleoceras*. Below: *Aphelops*. (Courtesy Texas Memorial Museum)

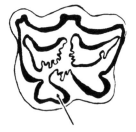 

Upper molar of *Equus* (left) and *Nannippus* (right). Nannippus has an isolated protocone which is characteristic of the hipparion horses.

swift, grazing animals having single hooves and living on open grasslands. As woodlands became prairie, the three toes that were useful to early horses for walking on matted vegetation and wet ground became a single hoof that was more efficient for running on open terrain. The two side toes became progressively more reduced until they no longer touched the ground and, as in modern horses, were finally reduced to small bony vestiges hidden under the skin. Legs became modified for swift running to elude predators on open plains. Low-crowned (brachydont) teeth suitable for browsing changed to high-crowned (hypsodont) teeth with heights of five or six inches, that would stand up to increased wear from abrasive grasses. And the teeth became more complex and molar-like to grind the tougher fodder.

Among the small three-toed horses from the early Miocene, *Parahippus*, about the size of a greyhound, was present in such great numbers at the Thomas Farm Site that a complete skeleton has been assembled. The somewhat larger primitive browser *Anchitherium* is also found at Thomas Farm. *Anchitherium* crossed the Bering bridge and colonized Eurasia.

A varied group of three-toed horses, present in Florida during the last half of the Miocene, is called the hipparion horses. The hipparions include *Hipparion, Cormohipparion, Neohipparion,* and *Nannippus.* Their teeth resemble those of the genus *Equus* which was the familiar Pleistocene horse, but the hipparions can usually be distinguished from *Equus* by the presence of an isolated little island of enamel called the protocone, present in the upper molars.

Pseudhipparion, a very small three-toed horse that lived 5 to 12 million years ago, is particularly interesting because much of its evolution occurred in Florida. *Pseudhipparion* survived two or three million years longer in Florida than in the Great Plains. Two late Miocene horses that began to look more like modern horses were *Astrohippus* and *Dinohippus.* Both had reduced or absent side toes and *Dinohippus* was probably the ancestor of *Equus.*

The pig-like animals (entelodonts) found in Florida begin with the "giant hog" *Dinohyus.* It had a body over ten feet long and is only found in the earliest Miocene deposits. Much more common are the peccaries (family Tayassuidae) which are found throughout the Florida Miocene. Peccaries are generally smaller than true pigs and have vertical canine tusks. *Desmathyus* appears first in the fossil record at Thomas Farm, some 18 million years ago. A large species of *Platygonus* and a long-jawed peccary called *Prosthenops* are present in the late

Miocene. Modern pigs were introduced into North America from Europe by early settlers.

Camels (the Camelidae), like horses, had their most extensive evolutionary history in North America. Their teeth, described as selenodont, had four crescent-shaped cusps. So far as is known, early camels had no hump.

Early Miocene camelids in Florida were *Floridatragulus* and *Nothokemas*, both from Thomas Farm. As the Miocene progressed, camels diversified into three tribes:

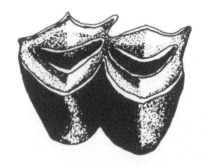

A selenodont tooth.

1. *Aepycamelus*, the largest, was a giraffe-like camel that stood 12 feet high at the shoulder. This long-necked creature was able to reach tender foliage far above the other browsers.
2. *Procamelus*, a medium-sized camel, and the very large *Megatylopus*, were both forerunners of modern camels.
3. *Hemiauchenia* was ancestral to modern llamas. The camelids were much reduced at the end of the Miocene and only *Hemiauchenia* made it through the Pliocene.

Ruminant animals related to deer and antelopes (also with selenodont teeth) were present fairly early in the Miocene. Represented by two tiny forms, *Blastomeryx* and *Machaeromeryx*, they were no larger than jackrabbits. At a late Miocene site in the Withlacoochee River is found *Pseudoceras*, a small hornless deer so primitive that it was formerly mistaken for a camel. A few years ago an unusual bent-horned beast was discovered by amateurs and given the name of *Kyptoceras amatorum*. It was the largest and last of an extinct family, the Protoceratidae.

As the Miocene drew to a close, an ice mass built up in the southern hemisphere and temperature and sea level dropped throughout the world. Resultant seasonal droughts and lowered water tables brought about the extinction of a great variety of animals, particularly decimating the hoards of land mammals. But the peninsula of Florida, extending into the warm waters of the tropics, offered refuge to many late Miocene animals. Several groups, including some hipparion horses, the protoceratids, and the crocodilian *Gavialosuchus*, survived longer in Florida than anywhere else in North America.

Glyptotherium dermal plate

The Pliocene and Pleistocene

The **Pliocene** began 5 million years ago and lasted 3.2 million years. The **Pleistocene** began 1.8 million years ago and lasted 1.7 million years, bringing us to within 10,000 years of the present.

As a result of more accurate dating methods, the time interval called the Ice Age is now known to span both the Pliocene and Pleistocene, a period of some 4.9 million years. Both epochs will therefore be described together.

The Ice Age began in earnest in Plio-Pleistocene time. Glaciers formed, then melted, and sea level fell and rose. The ocean probably came up only 15 to 20 feet (5 to 7 meters) above today's level, but it dropped to 300 feet (100 meters) below it. This didn't happen just four times as previously thought; from the late Miocene through the Pleistocene the sea advanced and retreated some *thirty* times. When the ice masses melted, seas covered all the low coastal parts of the peninsula. During glacial times the sea retreated, doubling the land area of Florida. This fluctuating shoreline explains why terrestrial fossils of the Pliocene and Pleistocene are found many miles out in the Gulf of Mexico and why marine deposits are found inland.

During glacial periods, temperatures plummeted over most of the world and parts of North America were literally uninhabitable. But Florida fared well during these extremes. Glaciers never got any closer than southern Illinois, about 500 miles (800 kilometers) to the north. In Florida, interglacial temperatures were probably a little warmer than present-day temperatures and glacial times only slightly colder. The sea surrounding Florida acted as a temperature buffer, storing the sun's heat energy and warming the cold air masses that pushed down from the north.

During interglacial times, Florida's terrain and vegetation were probably much like that found in unaltered areas of the state today. Glacial intervals, however, were considerably drier. When the sea level was low, a wide savanna extended from the Florida west coast along the Gulf of Mexico to the Caribbean coast of Mexico and Yucatan and thence to South America. Animal dispersal

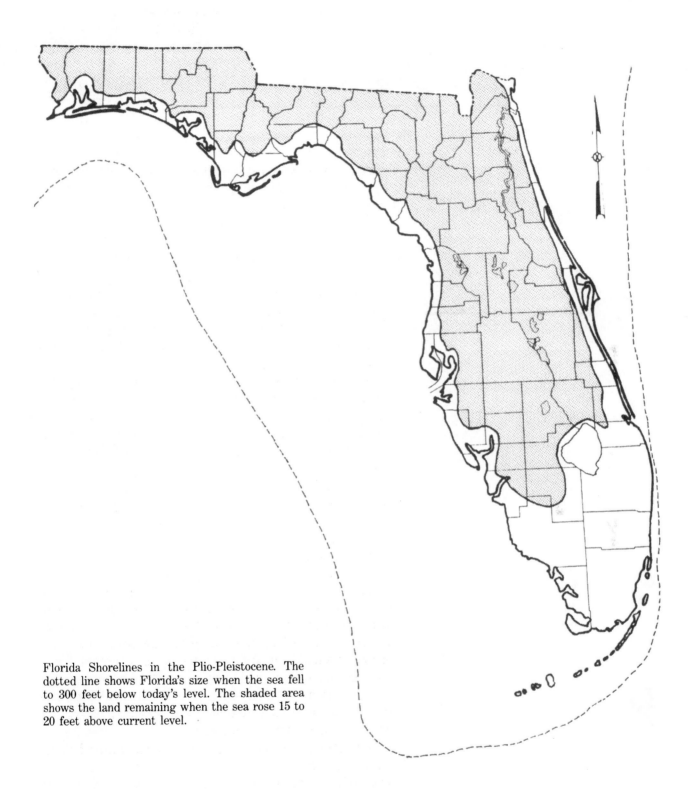

Florida Shorelines in the Plio-Pleistocene. The dotted line shows Florida's size when the sea fell to 300 feet below today's level. The shaded area shows the land remaining when the sea rose 15 to 20 feet above current level.

in both directions along this corridor, to and from South America, is known as the Great American Faunal Interchange. It began in the late Pliocene and has recurred, especially during glacial intervals, up to the present. This coastal plain also provided an avenue of migration into Florida for animals of western North America.

When sea level was high, the coastal corridor was flooded and creatures could enter Florida only from the north, limiting newcomers to animals found in eastern North America. North America was linked to Eurasia during glacial periods when sea level was low, but since this bridge was arctic in character, it could only be crossed by cold-adapted creatures.

Life was abundant in the Plio-Pleistocene seas. Several late Miocene marine formations extended into the Pliocene. Some Bone Valley deposits are topped off with Pliocene layers, both marine and terrestrial. The Tamiami Formation overlapped a million or so years into the Pliocene.

Also during the Pliocene, and perhaps extending into Pleistocene times, a remarkable marine deposit formed in the coastal waters of south Florida. These fossil shells were first described in 1887 by Angelo Heilprin, a naturalist who explored the Caloosahatchee River. Heilprin wrote:

> "This is without a doubt the most remarkable fossiliferous deposit that has yet been discovered in the state, and, from a purely paleontological standpoint, perhaps the most significant in the entire United States east of the Mississippi River. The fossils . . . crop out in almost countless numbers and attract attention, apart from their prodigious development, by their great variety, large size, and beautiful state of preservation."

These beds were subsequently named the Caloosahatchee Formation. They are found in excavations from Pinellas to Collier counties along the Gulf coast, and extend inland to Lake Okeechobee. This richly fossiliferous "shell hash" includes mollusks, barnacles, corals, and echinoids that lived on a tropical sea bottom at water depths from a few inches to 80 feet. All are remarkably preserved, sometimes retaining original color and luster. Only about 50 percent of these forms are still living today.

The Ice Age had profound effects on invertebrate marine life. There was a tremendous extinction of mollusks in the western Atlantic and Gulf of Mexico during the Plio-Pleistocene as a result of the falling temperature of the sea.

During the Pleistocene, the Fort Thompson Formation was deposited on top of the Caloosahatchee Formation in many areas. It is a mixture of fairly recent marine mollusks and freshwater limestone. At the southern tip of Florida, true coral reefs grew in the warm waters of the Caribbean. Today their remains, mixed with mollusks and echinoids, are found compacted into the Key Largo Limestone, which forms the foundation of the upper Florida Keys.

Two other Pleistocene formations are the Miami Oolite in Dade and Monroe counties, and the Anastasia Formation along the eastern coast of Florida. Miami Oolite has become an excellent ground water reservoir, and the Anastasia Formation, coquina rock used in the construction of early forts, proved to be superior material for stopping cannon balls. But neither offers much in the way of fossils.

Sharks, rays, and bony fish are abundant in Plio-Pleistocene marine deposits and closely resemble extant species.

Marine mammals were represented by more modern forms. Of the sea cows (Order Sirenia), dugongs disappeared from Florida at the end of the Miocene and the new sirenians were the familiar manatees, genus *Trichechus*. Long-beaked dolphins disappeared in the Pliocene and toothed whales similar to the sperm whale grew more common. The baleen (whalebone) whales became the true giants that we know today.

Although Florida never again had the diversity of animals present in the Miocene times, the land creatures of the Plio-Pleistocene were indeed wonderful. And as we approach the present day, the abundance of fossils increases dramatically. Older deposits are not only buried beneath younger ones, but erosion by rivers, rain, and sea has carried away or destroyed much of the early material. There are only one or two pockets of Oligocene fossils in Florida, but Pleistocene fossils can be found in every county.

Pliocene fossils are abundant in the Bone Valley Formation, although faunas range from late Miocene into the Pliocene. The Peace River passes through Bone Valley deposits, mixing Pliocene fossils with those of Pleistocene age. The Santa Fe River contains Pliocene fossil sites, also mixed with Pleistocene material in some places.

Pleistocene fossils are found throughout the state, but the type of deposit varies with the terrain. In North Florida and along the peninsula's central ridge, fossils are concentrated in sinkhole and cave deposits. River and stream sites are commonest from the central ridge to the

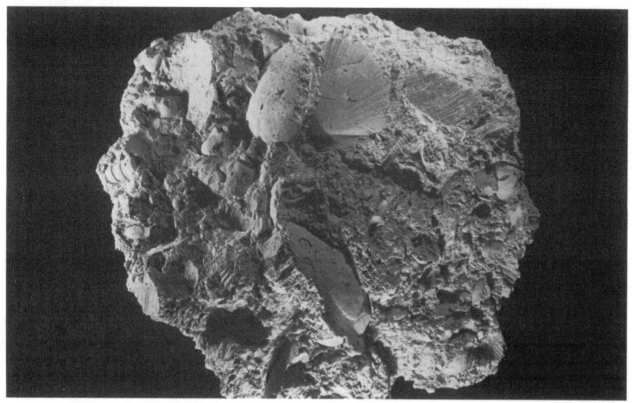

Tamiami Formation.

Caloosahatchee Formation.

Key Largo Limestone

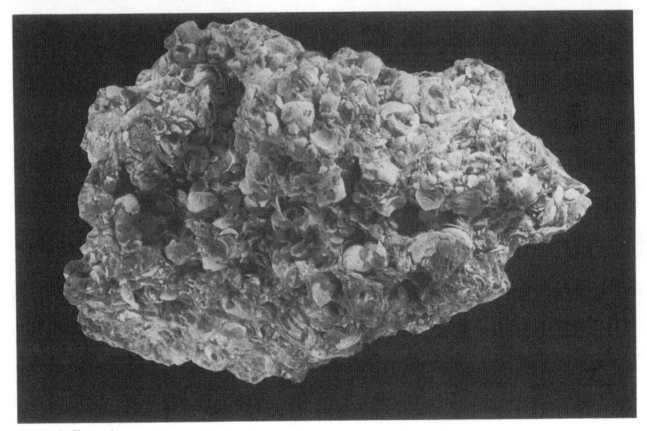

Anastasia Formation.

coast. Along the coast, fossils are found in areas that were once marsh and intracoastal waterways.

Pliocene-Pleistocene reptiles were essentially the same species as those present today. The crocodile *Gavialosuchus* became extinct and there were no more crocodiles in Florida until recent times. The big land tortoise *Geochelone* was present in the Pliocene and disappeared from North America in the late Pleistocene.

Birds are represented by an increasing number of extant species. Florida's most remarkable Pliocene bird was *Titanis walleri*, a predatory flightless creature that stood 10 feet tall and had its closest relatives in South America.

Some of the strangest mammals that arrived in Florida in Plio-Pleistocene times were the edentates from South America — sloths, armadillos and glyptodonts. The ground sloth *Glossotherium*, about the size of a large bull, appeared in the Pliocene, and the giant sloth *Eremotherium* came in the Pleistocene. *Eremotherium* grew to 20 feet in length and was the largest land animal ever to live in Florida.

Sloths were browsers and had huge claws; their large hypsodont teeth were rather simple and lacked enamel. Glyptodonts, armored beasts that resembled army tanks, reached Florida in the Pliocene. *Glyptotherium* was about the size of a Volkswagen "bug" and ate coarse vegetation. The polygonal bony plates that formed *Glyptotherium*'s armor are common fossil finds.

Other edentates included a big armadillo, *Dasypus bellus*, about twice the size of the armadillo common in Florida today, and the chlamythere *Holmesina*, an armadillo-like animal that was six feet long. The bony armor of both is frequently found.

Rodents prospered in the Plio-Pleistocene. *Geomys*, the pocket gopher, and *Sigmodon*, a cricetid rat, appeared for the first time. Progressive species changes in both these rodents are distinctive time indicators. Florida was home to a giant beaver in the Plio-Pleistocene. This huge rodent, *Castoroides ohioensis*, was about the size of a black bear. Another large rodent was the capybara *Hydrochoerus*, present in the Pleistocene. *Hydrochoerus* survives in South America today and is the world's largest living rodent, reaching a weight of 110 lbs (50 kg). An extinct capybara, *Neochoerus*, was half again as large as *Hydrochoerus*. Capybara teeth have distinctive parallel enamel plates and may reach several inches in length.

Some interesting carnivores developed during the Plio-Pleistocene epochs. Of the hyenoid dogs, *Osteoborus* disappeared at the end of the Miocene to be replaced by

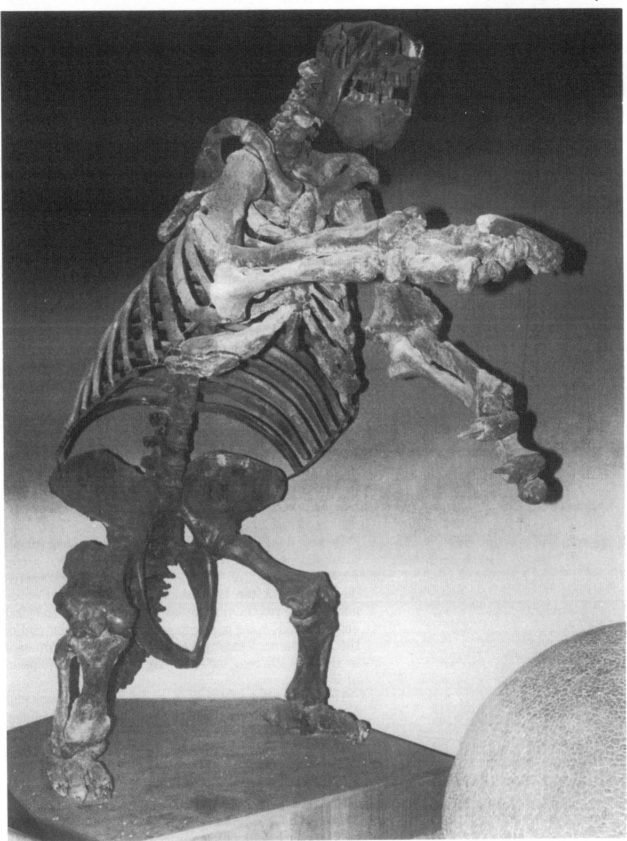

Eremotherium skeleton. (Courtesy Museum of Arts and Sciences in Daytona)

Borophagus in the Pliocene. The genus *Canis*, which contains modern dogs, wolves, and coyotes, appeared in the Pliocene. *Canis lepophagus*, a Pliocene coyote, later evolved into *Canis latrans*, the modern coyote. *Canis latrans* was common in Florida during the Pleistocene. The fierce Pleistocene dire wolf *Canis dirus* was as much as 20 percent larger than the modern gray wolf.

The short-faced bears, genera *Arctodus* and *Tremarctos*, evolved in the new world and inhabited Florida in both the Pliocene and Pleistocene. *Tremarctos floridanus* was a massive bear and was probably herbivorous. Its close relative *Tremarctos ornatus* survives in South America today as the Andean spectacled bear. True bears, genus *Ursus*, appeared in the Pliocene and survive to the present. They entered North America from Eurasia.

The otters, *Lutra*, appeared in the Pliocene and continue to enjoy themselves in Florida's streams and canals today.

Smilodon, the largest and most advanced of the sabertoothed cats, first appeared in the Pliocene as a smaller form called *Smilodon gracillis*. The late Pleistocene sabercat *Smilodon floridanus* grew to the size of a modern lion and bore upper canines modified into deadly blades measuring nine inches in length. *Smilodon's* lower jaw dropped far down, freeing the sabers in the upper jaw for stabbing prey.

The genus *Felis*, which contains modern cats, appeared in Florida in the Pliocene. Even larger than *Smilodon* was *Felis atrox*, a giant Pleistocene lion that was 50 percent larger than any living lion.

Despite interesting new faces among the proboscidians, diversity declined. Gomphotheres grew sparse: *Gomphotherium* and all the shovel-tusked gomphotheres disappeared at the beginning of the Pliocene. *Cuvieronius*, a gomphothere with short lower tusks and a spiral enamel band on its upper tusks, survived to the end of the Pleistocene. *Cuvieronius* spread into South America in the late Pliocene, after having most of its evolution in Florida.

The genus *Pliomastodon* appeared in the Pliocene and led to the Pleistocene genus *Mammut*, which includes the American mastodon. Mastodons had low skulls with strong upper tusks and vestigial lower tusks. Their teeth resemble those of gomphotheres but are simpler, lacking conules in the valleys between cusps. Mastodons became extinct at the end of the Pleistocene. Mammoths, genus *Mammuthus*, had huge upper tusks, high skulls and no lower tusks. Mammoths were present in Florida only

Painting of a herd of Mammoths in South Florida. (Courtesy Chris Kreider)

Proboscidian teeth

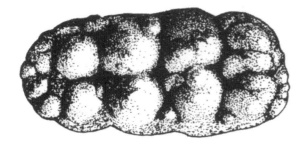

Gomphothere tooth.

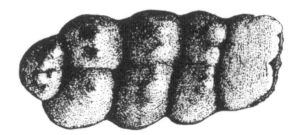

Mastodon tooth.

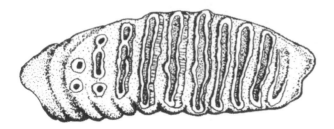

Early Pleistocene mammoth tooth.

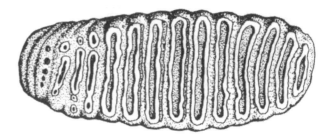

Late Pleistocene mammoth tooth.

during the Pleistocene and are characteristic index fossils of the epoch. Some mammoths grew to be 13 feet (4 meters) tall at the shoulder.

Mammoth teeth are composed of plates of enamel, dentine, and cementum which wear at different rates, so that the grinding surface is always rough for efficient crushing of vegetation. Late Pleistocene mammoth teeth have more plates than those from the early part of the epoch. Fragments of tusks and teeth of mastodons and mammoths are common fossil finds in Florida. Both animals survived until about 10,000 years ago and were still in Florida when early man arrived.

The many three-toed horses found in the Miocene disappeared at the start of the Pliocene. The exception was the gazelle-horse *Nannippus* which survived to the end of the Pliocene. *Equus*, the genus of modern horse, made its first appearance in the Pliocene and flourished for four million years. *Equus* teeth are present in almost every Pleistocene fossil deposit in Florida. It is fortunate that *Equus* emigrated across the Bering land bridge to Europe about 1.5 million years ago. In Europe and Asia, horses survived until the present, but they completely disappeared from North America at the end of the Pleistocene. *Equus* returned to this continent with the Spanish explorers.

Tapirs, rather peculiar-looking browsing animals, are related to rhinos and horses. They have down-curved noses and lived in Florida from the late Miocene through the Pleistocene. Tapirs survive today only in Asia and South America. Tapir teeth have distinctive pyramid-shaped cusps and are found mostly in Pleistocene fossil localities.

Two late Miocene rhinoceroses, *Teleoceras* and *Aphelops*, became extinct in the latest Miocene. Thereafter, there were no more rhinoceroses in Florida — or in North America.

Two genera of peccaries, *Platygonus* and *Mylohyus*, were very common in Florida during the Plio-Pleistocene. They are useful environmental indicators: *Mylohyus* was a forest dweller and *Platygonus* preferred grasslands. Though peccaries disappeared from Florida at the end of the Pleistocene, they are still alive and well in South and Central America, and a few remain in Arizona and Texas.

North America is the home continent for camels. Most of the varied Miocene camelids were gone by the Pliocene, but *Hemiauchenia* survived through the Pleistocene. *Palaeolama* appeared in the early Pleistocene, probably reentering Florida from South America after camelids colonized that continent in the

Pliocene. True camels also crossed the Bering Strait to Eurasia and Africa where they survive today. Llama-like camels that invaded South America are still there. But by the end of the Pleistocene, no camels remained in North America.

Interesting and varied antilocaprids continued to occur during the Pliocene. *Hexameryx*, a large six-horned antelope-like beast, is found only in the Pliocene of Central Florida. Other rare multi-horned antilocaprids vanished by late Pliocene and were replaced by a four-horned genus, *Capromeryx*, which continued through the Pleistocene. Primitive deer (cervids) appeared in earliest Pliocene, and by late Pliocene the commonest cervid was *Odocoileus*, indistinguishable from the modern white-tailed deer *Odocoileus virginianus*, living in Florida today.

The bovids (muskoxen, goats, and sheep) evolved in Eurasia and immigrated to North America in the Pleistocene. The only one to spread extensively into Florida was the genus *Bison*, which arrived in the late Pleistocene. *Bison* is a good time indicator, having evolved through three species over the last half million years: *Bison latifrons* had horns spanning six feet; *Bison antiquus'* horns were shorter; and shortest is the modern species, *Bison bison* (known to us as the buffalo). The three species can't be distinguished except by the size of the horn cores. Even more important, the teeth of small *Bison* are virtually indistinguishable from those of a modern cow, *Bos*, which was brought to the New World from Europe by early settlers.

Causes for Animal Extinction in Florida

Why did so many species of animals come to an end over the last 10 million years? What caused the periodic devastation of animal life that so dramatically punctuates Florida's past? These are tantalizing questions and the answers are far from complete.

The greatest number of extinctions occurred about five million years ago at the close of the Miocene when more than 60 genera of land mammals disappeared from North America. The time over which this loss occurred is not precisely known, but the process was not sudden. Changes in climate certainly brought an end to many groups of animals. Increasing cold and drought, even though interspersed with warmer interglacial cycles, destroyed Florida's lush tropical forests and with them, the browsing animals that were dependent on forest vegetation. Loss of the herbivores meant extinction of the carnivores that preyed upon them. Invading species from the north were often better adapted to Florida's new cold arid terrain than the animals already living there, and competition for food and habitat brought extinction to many previous residents.

The second event that extensively destroyed animal life happened rather suddenly at the end of the Pleistocene, about ten thousand years ago, when over 40 genera became extinct. Climatic change again played a large part in these extinctions. Many Pleistocene beasts that disappeared from Florida survive today in the tropics.

About ten thousand years ago, one of the new species that invaded Florida was *Homo sapiens*. Man was by then a skilled hunter and we know that he killed bison, horses, and mammoths. The aggressive hunting of large game by early man has been called "the Pleistocene overkill." But whether man, climatic change, or a combination of the two produced the sweeping extinctions of the late Pleistocene is still a matter of lively debate.

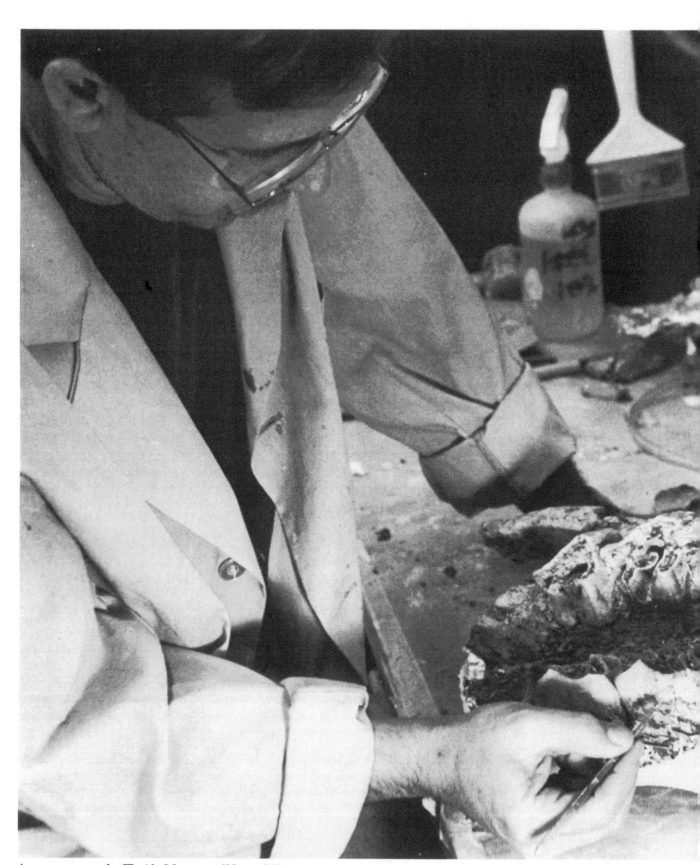

A preparator at the Florida Museum of Natural History at work on an opened plaster jacket.

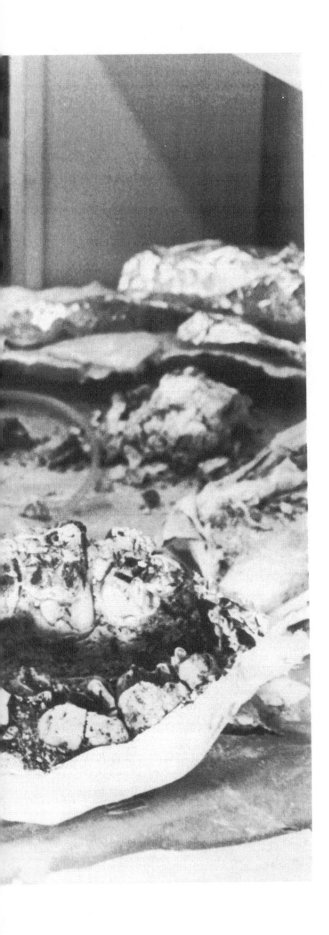

Pseudemys scute

CHAPTER 8

The Importance of Fossils

The Importance of Fossils

The remains of Florida's eventful life history have surprising applications to life today. Some fossil materials such as limestone, phosphate, and oil are used directly. Equally important, however, is the use of fossils as indicators for the detection and mapping of important resources. Finally, the fossil record traces life and the conditions necessary for life in this corner of the world through the sweeping environmental changes of 45 million years. Since environmental changes are occurring faster today then ever before in Florida's history, this last application may prove the most important of all.

Fossil Time Indicators

Because the fossil record is continuous since the beginning of life on earth, the development of animals can be traced from the earliest to the most recent and the timespan over which many animals lived can be determined. Fossils, then, can be used as time indicators. For example, the primitive three-toed horses that moved in after Florida emerged from the sea some 28 million years ago in the Oligocene, can be traced through various stages of development to the highly specialized horses of the late Pleistocene, which were similar to the modern horse *Equus*. From studying horse development and carefully dating major changes, we know that sites containing teeth of an intermediate genus of horse, *Nannippus*, must be at least two million years old. Often a group of fossils from animals that lived over a definite time range can be used to establish the age of a deposit with considerable accuracy. These are called "index fossils." A site having bones and teeth of *Mammuthus*, *Bison*, and *Equus* would indicate a late Pleistocene age: about 500,000 to 10,000 years.

Fossil Indicators of Geographic Change

Florida has been repeatedly covered by the sea, and the fossil record dramatically follows the changes in geography that resulted. For example, during the Pliocene and Pleistocene (the Ice Age), the sea rose and fell and glaciers repeatedly covered the northern part of this continent. As a result of these sea level changes, much of peninsular Florida alternated between sea bottom and dry land. Fossil layers deposited during a typical interglacial-glacial sequence might begin with a stratum containing deep water shells and fish. As the climate got colder, more of the earth's oceans were locked up in glaciers and the sea level fell. The deep sea bottom then became a bay; crabs and shallow water mollusks were

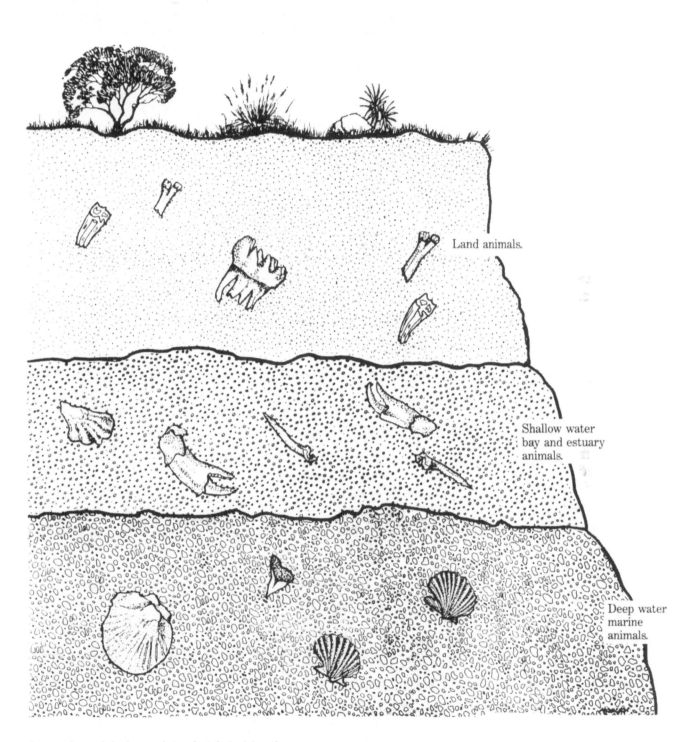

Land animals.

Shallow water
bay and estuary
animals.

Deep water
marine
animals.

Layers formed during an interglacial-glacial cycle.

abundant, and their remains formed the next layer of fossils. The sea fell further and the bay became land: an open plain inhabited by herds of grazing animals. As these animals died, their bones and teeth formed the topmost fossil layer. These events were repeated many times as the polar ice masses waxed and waned and sea level rose and fell.

Fossil Indicators of Climate

Fossils can give useful information about past environmental conditions. Temperature and rainfall are good examples.

An ancient sea bottom that contains several species of warm water corals gives good evidence of a warm sea at the time corals were alive. If the shallow sea that contained the corals was warm, land surrounded by the sea was probably warm, too.

Fossils of browsing animals that needed abundant rainfall for lush forage indicate a wet climate. Fossil land tortoises that required low grasses and sandy soil suggest a dry terrain.

The Economics of Fossils

Florida's fossil products have considerable market value.

Fossil limestones are mined for everything from roadbed material to ornamental building stone. Limerock heated in kilns is transformed into cement, plaster, and fertilizers.

The valuable phosphate deposits of Florida are fossil-related, though the riddle of what organisms produced them has yet to be solved. The probable source is the upwelling of sea bottom ooze composed of phosphate-containing micro-organisms. But exactly what happened in the late Miocene to cause the deposition of phosphate, not only in Florida but in many parts of the world, is still unclear.

In oil exploration, microfossils such as foraminifera are essential in subsurface mapping of both land and offshore deposits. And the oil itself comes from fossil micro-organisms.

Finally, individual fossils have become valuable. Rare and beautiful vertebrate fossils have an actual market value and are sought by collectors from as far away as Japan.

As a result, specimens that could provide vital links in Florida's fossil record are sometimes sold for profit. When valuable fossils become objects of decor for wealthy collectors, they are not available to science for study purposes, and are lost to the systematic record of life on this planet.

Fossils and the Future

World change continues. Man is altering his environment at an unprecedented rate. Atmospheric carbon dioxide has increased 29% since the beginning of the industrial revolution. Sea level has risen one to two millimeters per decade over the past 100 years. Certainly the low, flat peninsula of Florida will be greatly changed. The knowledge of Florida's past experiences with a rising sea and warming climate can help prepare for what is ahead.

The study of fossils not only reveals wonderful creatures long vanished from the earth, but it gives us glimpses into the past in which these animals lived: how they flourished and why they died. Such glimpses make us better able to understand our present world and predict its future.

Museum Collections

The official compiler of Florida's fossil record is the Paleontology Department of the Florida Museum of Natural History in Gainesville. Fascinating activities go on in this place. Fossils come in from amateur and professional excavations all over the state. Each specimen is cleaned, repaired, and labeled with a number. For each, a computer file is kept, noting the name of the animal, the material (such as rib or tusk), the locality from which it was collected, the formation that it came out of, and the data collected. If enough bones of a particular animal are recovered, the entire skeleton may be reconstructed.

Information and casts of fossil material are exchanged with paleontologists all over the world. Accounts of new fossil finds are published and with new information, the classification of fossil creatures is enlarged and revised. Maps are prepared showing places where fossils have been found and the formations they came from are correlated with similar formations around the world. Ancient animal populations in Florida are compared with similar animals elsewhere, often revealing patterns of migration and causes for extinction.

Gradually the picture of life is assembled.

For the museum visitor, there are exhibits depicting fossil sites, methods of fossil restoration, and what some of the animals and their enviorments may have looked like.

But for those who search for fossils, the museum offers — and asks — more.

Paleontology is uniquely dependent on amateur fossil hunters both for acquiring specimens and for locating new collecting sites. Limited time, manpower, and budget prevent wide ranging exploration by museum personnel. But amateurs are numerous and they go everywhere. Many of the important fossil sites which Florida paleontologists have excavated over the past two decades were discovered by amateurs. Countless valuable specimens have been donated by amateurs, specimens that improve knowledge of existing animals or reveal animals previously unknown. Some species have been named for the amateur discoverer. *But keep in mind that for a fossil to be of any value to a museum collection, exact notes on where it was found are essential.*

Collecting fossils on state lands in Florida (which includes all navigable waterways and offshore waters) requires a Fossil Collecting Permit issued by the Florida Program of Vertebrate Paleontology. For more information about the fossil collecting permit see Appendix A.

In return for assistance from amateurs, the Florida Museum of Natural History (FMNH) offers several services:

1. Help with fossil identification. Material must have enough features to permit identification, however. A fragment of limb bone without either end offers no clues to even a professional paleontologist. The museum describes this service:

Personnel of the Division of Vertebrate Paleontology of the Florida Museum of Natural History will identify fossils that have been legally collected or purchased. To aid our identifications, tell us where the specimen was found, to the best of your knowledge. Our greatest expertise lies with specimens from Florida and the rest of the Southeast, and from the Caribbean region. We recommend you look elsewhere for help with specimens from outside of these regions. There are three basic methods we prefer:

Electronic Images. Send us digital images of specimens either as e-mail attachments in JPEG format (to rhulbert@flmnh.ufl.edu) or post them on your own web site and e-mail us the address (URL) of the site. Please include a ruler or some other indication of scale in the image. Take pictures of more than one side of the specimen.

Bring the specimens to Dickinson Hall. Those in the Gainesville area can bring their specimens directly to us. We are located on the UF campus on Museum Road, just up the hill from the Shands Hospital/Research complex. You will need a temporary permit to park on campus. We recommend that you call or e-mail us and make an appointment, as sometimes all our personnel are out in the field or otherwise unavailable. Our phone number is (352) 392–1721 x 259. When reaching Dickinson Hall, go in the front doors and ask the receptionist to page us. Available hours are M–F, 9–5.

Mailing Specimens. Mail or ship specimens to:

Div. of Vertebrate Paleontology
Florida Museum of Natural History
Dickinson Hall, Univ. of Florida
Gainesville, FL 32611-7800

Pack fossils as you would fragile china. We recommend wrapping each specimen individually in bubble-wrap or soft paper, placing them inside a padded box, then put the boxes with specimens in a larger, sturdy box cushioned with packing material. Make sure to include a return address and phone number within the package. We are not responsible for damage done in transit both to and from the museum.

We are happy to provide this service to the public. For large collections (more than 10 specimens), we ask that you make a voluntary contribution, to offset the time involved, to the VP Research Fund in the UF Foundation. It supports field work to collect fossils throughout Florida.

2. Seminars and meetings. The FMNH cooperates with the Florida Paleontology Society (FPS), an organization of amateurs interested in fossils, hosting meetings, providing speakers, and organizing field trips. The FPS website is www.flmnh.ufl.edu/orgs/club.htm.

3. The FMNH Newsletter. Many articles are written by the FMNH staff. It is mailed to FPS members on a regular basis.

4. The publication *Contributions to Florida Paleontology*. A semi-scientific series on new fossil discoveries produced by the FPS.

5. The maintenance of an excellent website: www.flmnh.ufl.edu.

In few endeavors do amateurs and professionals work together so closely as in paleontology in Florida.

Collecting fossils in a South Florida shell pit.

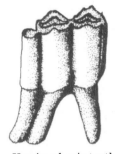

Hemiauchenia tooth

CHAPTER 9

Safety,
Courtesy,
and
the Law

Before beginning your fossil explorations, take a minute to read the rules and appreciate the hazards of the game.

Your success as a fossil finder will depend a lot on being able to get permission to hunt good sites. Your well-being and perhaps your survival will depend on the safety precautions you take. The following tips are offered to help with both.

Safety

1. Never hunt alone. Though such places as quarries and rivers may seem serene, they can be hazardous. Safe SCUBA diving always requires working in pairs. Hunting with a friend is more fun anyway.
2. Stick to shallow rivers and streams unless you are a strong swimmer. Silt from the bottom can blind your vision. Swiftly flowing rivers are treacherous.
3. Leave the exploration of sinks, caves and underwater caves to the professionals. These sites kill even *trained* explorers every year.
4. Take first aid equipment and drinking water along in the car and, on long treks, on your person.

Courtesy and Law

On state lands:
1. It is very important to know that fossil collectors who collect on state lands in Florida, which include all navigable waterways and offshore waters, are required to have a Fossil Collecting Permit issued by the Florida Program of Vertebrate Paleontology. See Appendix A for more information and a permit application.
2. In state and national parks, the removal of fossils (or any other natural material) is prohibited. Fortunately, fossil sites in state parks are usually in the rivers that flow through them. If you see good river fossils in the park, you can often find similar fossils if you hunt upstream or downstream, outside park boundaries.

On private lands:
1. Never trespass. Always get permission from land owners and pit operators. Florida's trespass penalties are severe. Above all, don't tamper with fences or gates. Cattlemen are unsympathetic with these offenses and prosecution is almost certain.

2. Ask permission courteously. The person in charge of a quarry may not believe that there is such a thing as a fossil; it is often best just to say you are looking for bones or shells. Explain that you will stay away from machinery and working crews. Many quarries are reluctant to admit visitors because of liability for a visitor's injury. Some require that you sign a waiver.

3. If you have permission:
   a. Always leave gates the way you found them.
   b. Don't litter.
   c. Stay away from machinery in active quarries and landfill operations.
   d. If the area is fenced, leave before the work crew starts closing up.

4. When you leave:
   a. Try to find someone to thank. Tell him it was great!
   b. If the hunting was good, ask permission to return.
   c. If he seems interested, show him what you've found. He may have good information about where there is more.

Hunting fossils on the Aucilla River.

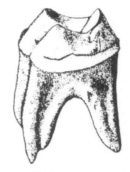

Tapirus tooth

CHAPTER 10

The Adventures of Fossil Hunters

The pursuit of Florida's fossils has taken hunters to out-of-the-way places for some wonderful discoveries. Careful detective work, ingenious recovery methods, single-minded devotion, self education, persistence, and blind luck — all have played a part in uncovering Florida's ancient past.

On the University of Florida campus, Dickinson Hall houses the extensive fossil collection. Row upon row of white metal cabinets fills the vast Paleontology Range. Each cabinet is labeled according to age and location and each is filled with fossils, many found by amateur collectors. Dr. S. David Webb, then-Associate Curator of Vertebrate Paleontology, stopped in front of a cabinet labeled "Santa Fe River" and pulled out a wide drawer. As he examined the dark brown bones, he reminisced about his introduction to the Santa Fe.

"When I came to Florida in 1964, I was fortunate to have Robert Allen and Jessie Robertson as lab technicians. Robert was an especially able SCUBA diver, as was his best friend, an amateur collector from Ocala, Ben Waller.

"Not long after my arrival, the four of us were camped at the Santa Fe River to excavate what was then the only site in eastern North America producing Pliocene land vertebrates. Together, Robert and Ben were the finest pair of SCUBA diving paleontologists I've ever seen. I could not have asked for a better introduction to Florida paleontology or SCUBA diving. Ben was the one who took me in tow with incredible patience, instructed me in the practices and precaution of SCUBA. The Pliocene fossils came from a rather deep hole in the river where the water was as dark as black tea. The first time down, I became disoriented and claustrophobic before my eyes had time to adapt. And Ben, being a perfect instructor, motioned me back up and talked me through my initial panic. He pointed out that you could always follow your bubbles up if you wished, but that the unique fossils on the bottom were worth staying down for. I will never forget the thrill, during the next hour, of finding my first Pliocene antelopes, horses, and giant beavers. And of course Ben was right there with his high sign, cheering each one I found and showing me each specimen he found.

"There are a lot of surprising things among the vertebrates of the Pliocene of the Santa Fe River. Over all, it's astonishing that the fauna is dominated by grassland specimens like *Capromeryx,* a small pronghorn antelope, and *Nannippus,* a three-toed horse with very high crowned teeth. The contrast with the massive mesic hammock that grows there now really sinks in when you sleep in those woods by night and collect in the

Pliocene by day.

"One of the unique specimens from the Santa Fe River is the palate of a true hyaenid, one of a handful of specimens proving that these Old World scavenger-predators were established in North America for about a million years. But the most remarkable find of all was Ben Waller's discovery of a giant predacious bird of the extinct family Phorusracidae, previously known only from South America. The Santa Fe bird is estimated to have stood ten feet tall and was a new genus and species which Pierce Brodkorb, our avian paleontologist, appropriately named *Titanis walleri*."

*   *   *

When Lewis Ober and Bill Weaver were graduate students at the University of Florida, Dr. Webb taught them about finding fossils in the sinkholes of north Florida.

Later, as faculty members of Miami-Dade Community College, Lew and Bill were delighted to learn that sinkholes are fairly common in the limestone of southeast Florida. The men felt certain that these natural animal traps were as full of fossils as were sinkholes in the northern part of the state. But there are two major difficulties with sinks in the Miami Oolite. First, the water table is not far below the surface, so by the time the fossil-bearing layers in the sinkhole are reached, workers are up to their knees in mud. Second, in populous Dade County, most sinks have been used for generations as refuse dumps. Fossils are well protected by layers of beer bottles and rusting automobiles. So information about untouched sinkholes in Monkey Jungle, a tourist attraction in southwest Dade County, came as exciting news to Lew and Bill.

Monkey Jungle is a fenced hammock laced with screened boardwalks that allow visitors access to observe a variety of primates. The spectators are caged, the monkeys are loose. Luckily, Monkey Jungle owner Frank DuMond was sympathetic to Bill and Lew's request to explore his land for animals of Florida's past.

The many solution holes in the Pleistocene limestone that floored the Monkey Jungle hammock were filled with black-brown muck peculiar to south Florida. But DuMond knew of one large hole that had been deeply excavated to form a home for alligators. A year earlier, a dragline using a "clamshell" bucket had cleaned out the sink and its contents had been placed in 15 neat piles. Lew Ober says, "When we first glimpsed the site, rains had washed away much of the sand and muck. Before our eyes lay pile after pile with exposed bones: bear teeth, peccary jaws, deer antler, and a fine scattering of the bones of frogs, snakes and rodents. What a find!"

With the help of students from Miami Dade Community College, Bill and Lew were able to work the piles thoroughly. Ignoring alligators and apes, the team screenwashed the piles through coarse and fine screens. Fossils were separated and bagged. Experts at the Florida Museum of Natural History and elsewhere helped with identification, and ultimately over 50 species of late Pleistocene animals were found.

Surprisingly, the huge Pleistocene lion, *Felis atrox*, previously known in Florida from a single skull found in the Itchetucknee River, turned up in this south Florida site, an indicator that the great cat once roamed the entire peninsula.

Much of the Monkey Jungle material now reposes in the study collection at the Florida Museum of Natural History in Gainesville, where the carefully conducted work of Lew Ober and Bill Weaver continues to yield valuable secrets of Florida's past.

*   *   *

At the opposite end of the state in Walton County, a row of ancient marine terraces drops from the red clay farmland of southern Alabama to the rich tidal flats of Choctowatchee Bay. The east-west-oriented terraces are furrowed from north to south by innumerable spring-fed creeks. In this beautiful panhandle county every Cenozoic Era known in Florida is exposed — from Eocene to Recent.

Wayne Wooten grew up on a hillside in Walton County. As a youngster he hunted the petrified wood that was uniquely abundant on his land. Wayne now has a Ph.D. in astronomy and teaches at the University of West Florida in Pensacola. But he still returns to Walton County to look for fossils.

In 1972 Wayne was "the" high school science teacher in Paxton, Florida, a little town on the Florida-Alabama line. Because of his love of the past, he offered the students of Paxton High School a special course called Florida Geology. The course was popular for many reasons, chief among them was its field trips.

One April morning Wayne drove the students south through the hills of Walton County, pointing out the terraces and changing age of the land about them. The field trip wound up at Camp Creek — a favorite fossil site. A short way below the spring from which the creek issues, the class waded into the shallow water and began exploring the bottom. The creek banks were a mass of pink and white bloom of mountain laurel, and the dozen or so ninth graders were in high spirits. An occasional shark tooth or turtle scute turned up, but the chief product of the hunt seemed to be a great deal of water soaked up by hilarious youngsters. No one appeared likely to win the ten extra credit points that had been offered for the trip's outstanding fossil find.

Suddenly there was a whoop of joy. "Horse! Look! Horse tooth!" The boy waving the muddy object had grown up on a farm and he knew his animals. There was no doubt about what he had found.

The discovery was unexpected to say the least. In the Miocene deposits of the panhandle, horse teeth are about as scarce as hens' teeth. And the finder was a student whose classroom standing was anything but outstanding. Despite his enthusiasm, his test scores left him poised between a D and an F.

But there it was, a perfect tooth of the three-toed horse *Merychippus*, lying in the hand of a boy grinning from ear to ear. As the dripping class crowded around to see, the finder of the horse tooth looked up and said, "I reckon I may pass this course yet!"

Wayne Wooten says yes, he passed.

*   *   *

Clifford Jeremiah, a soft-spoken, energetic physician, has hunted fossils around Jacksonville for more than 20 years. His interest in extinct animals has turned his patient waiting rooms into first class natural history museums. One room features enormous dinosaurs; the other bristles with the Ice Age animals of Florida, including the skeleton of a giant ground sloth that towers 15 feet above one corner.

But Cliff's real fascination is with sharks, particularly the extinct giant *Carcharodon megalodon*. When he began medical practice in Jacksonville in 1964, the St. Johns River was being extensively dredged. Often the whirling dredge bit would chew into a fossiliferous layer, and out of the huge pipe would pour the teeth of *C. megalodon* along with those of mako, tiger, and many other sharks. Most teeth were chipped or broken, but some were perfect. Cliff collected in person and also paid dredge workers to collect for him. When the dredge hit a good pocket, he would sometimes go home with 20 or 30 pounds of shark teeth.

Cliff had seen the impressive restoration of *C. megalodon* at the National Museum in Washington, and as his collection of fossil shark teeth grew, he decided to build his own life-size set of jaws of this monster shark, filling them with real teeth. In order to place the teeth accurately, he studied the limited information on fossil

Cliff Jeremiah.

The giant ground sloth in Cliff Jeremiah's waiting room.

shark anatomy. *Carcharodon megalodon*'s nearest relative, the modern great white shark *Carcharodon carcharias,* furnished the best clues about tooth shape and size variation.

Next he studied techniques of fossil restoration and duplication. He learned to use mold-making materials such as liquid latex and silicone compounds. He became skilled in fiberglass casting and learned to create surface texture and apply color with an airbrush. He learned to preserve fossil bone, to repair breaks and restore missing pieces. Then he began construction.

The tough fiberglass jaws Cliff made measure eight by nine feet. True to his high standard of accuracy, Cliff even reproduced the replacement rows of teeth that curve neatly around the inside of the jaw. Hundreds of teeth were used and the result is spectacular. The finished jaws gape ferociously from a mirrored display case in the clinic waiting room.

This versatile and talented fossil enthusiast has made copies of many Florida fossils, including a skeleton of the giant ground sloth *Eremotherium.* The sloth was collected by Don Serbousek, an equally dedicated fossil finder. Cliff and Don cooperated to make the model of the sloth. But that's the next story.

The jaws of the giant white shark.

* * *

In Ormond Beach, right on U.S. 1, is a little white shop with a huge rusting anchor outside. A sign with the diver's diagonal stripe identifies the building as Don's Dive Shop. Here Don Serbousek has taught SCUBA diving since 1959. And underwater Florida has in turn taught Don.

In the early 1960s when he was one of the first underwater explorers of the rivers and springs of central Florida, Don would occasionally find ancient animal bones and the artifacts of early man.

On a trip to the Little River, an isolated stretch of the Aucilla that rises from an underground limestone cavern and soon sinks into another, Don and two friends spotted several piles of bones and occasional Indian artifacts. The teeth of mammoth and mastodon were scattered between the bone piles in such abundance that the swimmers gathered and stacked them like cord wood!

When the team returned the following weekend, they brought SCUBA gear and began a careful inventory of what the river contained. They recovered two Indian bowls and some projectile points, and mapped several groups of bones. In a 20-foot-deep hole on the river bottom, their underwater lamps revealed the well preserved skeleton of a huge mastodon — identifiable by half

Don Serbousek recovering mastodon bones from
the Little River (above) and with the mastodon's
lower jaw (right).

of the lower jaw lying on top of a pile of leg bones! This find was worthy of their best efforts.

Several trips were needed to bring up the jaw and long bones. And lying in the sand beneath them was a row of vertebrae. Nearby were ribs, forelegs, shoulder blades, and the broken but complete pelvis. But there was no sign of the elephant's skull.

After the accessible bones had been brought up, the hunt for the skull began. "The water was dark," Don recalls, "and our lights weren't very good in those days. A lot of the hunting was done by feel. When I was fanning away the sand I found a flat rock, but I moved on. After a bit I thought, 'that's a funny rock. Everything else in this river is sharp — eroded and broken limestone.'" Don went back to find the rock again. It wasn't easy to find, but after a considerable hunt he felt it again. In fanning away more and more sand, the "rock" got bigger and bigger and began to curve downward. It was the skull, partially buried in a layer of blue clay, beneath the rest of the skeleton. There was nothing for it but to dig out the skull with dive knives.

Exposing the skull was a tedious job. Divers worked in pairs, using dive knives or garden trowels. The blue clay was slowly scooped out and moved aside. One tusk was still in the skull; the other tusk was uncovered nearby. At last the mass of bone was free enough to feel the teeth on its under-surface.

The team was confronted with the problem of how to bring the monster to the surface from a depth of 23 feet. They solved it with a framework of steel pipe laced with a floor of heavy canvas. Four deflated inner tubes were tied beneath the frame, one at each corner. They carefully eased the skull onto the raft and began to inflate the inner tubes. As the platform rose, the air within the inner tubes expanded and their lift increased. When the frame was about knee high, it got hard to manage. When it reached waist high, the whole thing began to tilt. The divers frantically tried to force it back down — too late! The raft shot out from under the skull, and the raft together with one of the divers went flying to the surface. The skull sank toward Don and another diver who were still on the bottom. They did their best to cushion its fall as they scrambled out of the way, but the mass of bone bounced when it hit the bottom. Miraculously, it was unharmed.

The divers surfaced and discussed the problem. They decided to tie four more inner tubes on the sides of the raft to pull rather than push. The skull was again maneuvered onto the raft and the new inner tubes were inflated with great care. Slowly, the team swam the raft

Don Serbousek's mastodon skull bouyed by inner tubes.

upward. When it hung about four feet beneath the surface the tubes underneath were inflated and the skull emerged from the water!

The uncooperative behavior of the beast earned it the name Priscilla. "Clearly," says Don, "it was a female."

A lot of planning went into Priscilla. Before her skull was brought out of the river, the men built a large tank and filled it with a water-soluble acrylic preservative. The skull was immediately placed in the tank and other of Priscilla's bones were placed around it. The solution was kept circulating with a small pump. As the bones soaked up the preservative, the concentration of the solution was increased until the skeleton was thoroughly hardened.

Don made many return trips to the site and found the other half of the lower jaw about eight inches beneath the surface of the blue clay. As the sand and clay were cleared away, hundreds of carved bone needles were found. Archaeologists speculate that the needles were used to weaken large animals before the kill.

There were no recognizable butcher marks on Priscilla's bones, but the team thinks that early man must have had something to do with her death. Perhaps a hunt drove her into the river where she slipped into the deep hole and drowned. "She was old," says Don. "She was on her last set of teeth and there's arthritis in her backbone."

Meticulous paleontology takes a great deal of perseverance; recovering Priscilla's skeleton took three years. Eventually, all but two of her vertebrae came to light. Finally, every scrap of bone was picked up. Don says, "We never found many tail vertebrae, though. I think an alligator must have chewed it off."

When all the bones were hardened and thoroughly dried, Don began to experiment with techniques to make an accurate copy of his mastodon. He tried a styrofoam casting technique, but the casts lacked accuracy and durability.

From other fossil enthusiasts, Don heard about a doctor from Jacksonville who was making remarkably fine replicas of fossils. Eventually Don Serbousek and Cliff Jeremiah came together at a Florida Paleontological Society meeting. They compared notes on methods of duplicating fossils and Cliff agreed to visit Don and Priscilla.

He watched as Don made a mold. It was part of a giant ground sloth which Don had found, nearly complete, some years before. Cliff was profoundly impressed by Don's fossil sloth but not by the mold-making. "That mold will be a bitch to get a cast out of," was Cliff's verdict.

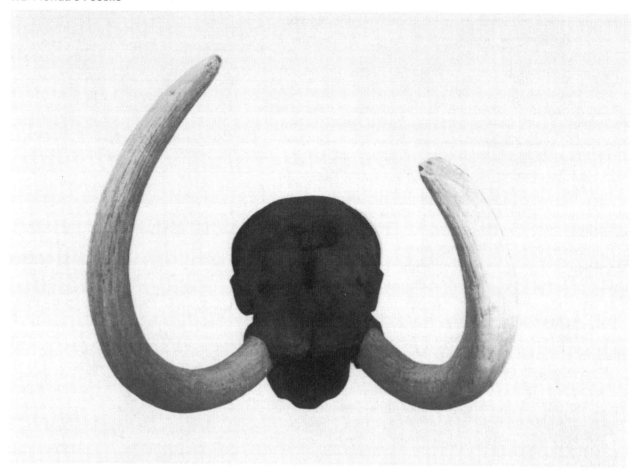

The replica of Priscilla's skull.

"It was, too," Don recalls.

The two men decided to pool their talents and Don suggested that they begin by copying the huge sloth, *Eremotherium.* The finished reproduction nearly touches the ceiling of Cliff's clinic waiting room.

The team of Jeremiah and Serbousek went on to duplicate countless other specimens — fossils they collected, fossils from other collectors, and museum specimens. After 11 years of collaboration, they began work on Priscilla.

The project, which took 22 years, is now complete and the original Priscilla (which turned out to be a male) now stands in the Florida Museum of Natural History. All those who worked on it are proud of the painstaking care that went into this piece of pioneer paleontology. But for Don Serbousek, it's a much more personal thing. He says simply, "There will never be another elephant like Priscilla."

* * *

There is one thing about fossil hunting that is certain: the more you hunt the more you find. Frank Garcia is a prime example.

Frank first found fossils at age eight, on the shores of Lake Okeechobee. In high school, he was nicknamed "the bone hunter." After high school, he worked in the asbestos trade for a living, but his real life was fossils. He searched river bottoms, canal banks, limerock quarries, and phosphate mines. On weekends Frank got up before dawn to hunt, often returning home long after dark. He spent summer evenings after work searching sites near his home south of Tampa. Over the past 20 years he estimates that his fossiling trips number over 3,000.

The devotion paid off. Frank found fossils — rare sea cows, rhinos, three-toed horses, long-beaked dolphins. He learned about Florida geology and ancient environments, about how animal skeletons fit together and how their bones change over millions of years. He made sketches of fossils that are common finds and published them as a field guide for other hunters. His knowledge and experience won him the status of field associate for the Smithsonian, and he has found and preserved fossil whales, sea cows, and dolphins for the famous institution. He has also located sites for the Florida Museum of Natural History and donated outstanding specimens.

And all along, Frank dreamed, like fossil hunters everywhere, of a really great find.

In the early 1970s a young boy named Jim Ranson showed Frank a few vertebrate fossils from a shell pit in southwest Hillsborough County. Frank visited the pit — and found a few bones. He didn't return until 1978. The second visit netted an enormous mastodon jaw. But an even more important find was a consistent yellowish sand layer with occasional land fossils and a sprinkling of garfish scales — evidence of an ancient stream channel. Frank returned at intervals as the shell mining operation uncovered more of this fossil-bearing stratum. In May of 1983, just before leaving on a fossil-collecting trip to Nebraska, Frank visited the pit and found a dramatic increase in the fossil bones exposed in the ancient stream layer. He predicted that within a year the Leisey pit would be a spectacular fossil site.

When he returned from Nebraska a month later, Frank couldn't wait to see what was happening at Leisey. It was pouring rain when he walked down to look at the bank where the fossil layer had been. The first indication that his prediction had come true came from piles of shell that had already been removed. They were laced with bone fragments. When he reached the floor of the pit and looked up

Frank Garcia.

at the fossil-bearing area, he saw what he had dreamed of finding: an 18-inch thick layer packed with incredible numbers of bones. Gleaming blue-black against the yellowish matrix were limb bones, jaws, skulls, teeth — a vast array of Florida's Pleistocene animals.

Frank and eight friends excavated Leisey for 110 consecutive days. "But on the Fourth of July holiday," says Frank, "I was the only person digging. I had a little American flag stuck up beside me, but I was digging. This was the find of a lifetime, I couldn't leave."

The owners of the Leisey pit generously arranged for paleontology and the digging of shell marl to co-exist for a while. Using earth-moving equipment from the quarry, they uncovered 1-1/2 acres of the fossil layer so that the bones could be further excavated by hand.

Paleontologists around the world were interested in the Leisey fossils. The Florida Museum of Natural History began studying the site. Nowhere in Florida had land animal bones been found in such quantity. There were llama-like camels, horses, tapirs, mammoths, mastodons, and a sabercat. And the state of preservation was superb! Study revealed that the animals lived about 1.5 million years ago in the first part of the Pleistocene in an area that was probably the mouth of a brackish river. The animals had died not far upstream from where their fossilized remains were found. Their bones apparently washed downstream to concentrate in an estuary where mangroves grew and shells were abundant.

The sheer number of fossils was staggering, but pit operations could not be suspended indefinitely. Money and manpower were needed to salvage the unique assemblage. The Florida Museum of Natural History wanted the bones badly but couldn't manage the excavation in the time available. So Frank enlisted the help of the Tampa Bay Mineral and Science Club — an organization of enthusiastic and knowledgeable amateurs. Money was raised and volunteers were found. Frank and his friend Mickey Fowler moved to the site for the duration of the dig.

Under the direction of Frank and the staff of the Florida Museum of Natural History, teams of volunteers worked carefully in a mapped grid, uncovering fossils, recording their position, then preserving and removing them. All finds were destined for the Division of Vertebrate Paleontology at the museum in Gainesville. Ultimately the museum received the equivalent of *two semi trailers* full of fossils.

People came from everywhere to help dig Leisey fossils. One family came all the way from Australia and a doctor flew down on weekends from Pennsylvania.

It will be years before the Leisey material yields its

Photographer Red Tincher kneels beside complete skeletons of horse and camel assembled by Frank Garcia and laid out on the Leisey shell marl.

entire story, but interesting and intriguing facts have already emerged. More than 140 species of animals have been identified. Of these, 40 are birds, mostly aquatic, and eight are new to science. The animals died at various times of life. Skeletons vary from the very young with incompletely formed bones, to aged individuals with worn teeth and arthritic joints. But for some reason almost all the elephants found were juveniles. The Leisey animals were the immediate ancestors of the famous Rancho La Brea fauna from the tar pits of California. The Leisey *Smilodon gracilis* was the predecessor of the huge sabercat *Smilodon floridanus.*

Probably the best thing about Leisey is the enormous number of bones—enough material to do in-depth studies of animals previously represented by only a few incomplete specimens.

All those hours that Frank Garcia spent looking for fossils have been richly rewarded. His discovery at Leisey will take its place in the history of paleontology as one of our most important windows on the past.

* * *

In the Paleontology Range of the Florida Museum of Natural History, the rows of white metal cabinets stretch into the shadowy recesses of the huge room. Associate Curator Dr. Bruce MacFadden says, "Now look on top of the cabinets."

From the vantage point of the top of a ladder, one sees trays of black bones entirely covering the cabinet tops. "Those are Leisey fossils. Every one of them will be identified, numbered, and added to the collection.

"Since this museum came into existence, Florida fossil hunters have contributed much," continues Dr. MacFadden. "Specimens they have donated, sites they have found, fossil digs they have helped with. More so than any other state I know of, talented and knowledgeable amateurs have built this collection along with the museum staff. Florida's fossil heritage is so rich that this is the way it should be. Those who hunt fossils should feel a great sense of pride in contributing to, and building, one of the top ten vertebrate collections in the United States. Because it is a state collection, it belongs to all of us."

Glossary

Amphibians. Frogs and salamanders.

Antilocaprids. Animals related to the modern antelopes.

Apertural. In mollusks, the side having the opening.

Aquatic. Living in the water.

Aragonite. A form of calcium carbonate that is frequently dissolved in the fossilization process. Many fossil mollusks and corals made of aragonite remain only as internal and external molds.

Articulated. Bones arranged in the same relationship as in the living animal.

Artiodactyls. The even-toed hoofed mammals such as camel, deer, and bison.

Assemblage. Group or collection.

Astragalus. The ankle bone in vertebrates that articulates with the tibia.

Aves. Birds.

Bivalves. (Class Bivalvia, formerly Pelecypoda.) Shells with two halves such as clams or scallops.

Bovids. Animals related to cattle and bison.

Brachyodont. Low-crowned tooth.

Browsers. Herbivores that eat predominantly trees and shrubs.

Calcite. A relatively stable form of calcium carbonate that is frequently little changed by fossilization. Oysters, barnacles, and echinoids are composed of calcite.

Camelids. Animals related to camels and llamas.

Canids. Animals related to dogs and wolves.

Cannon Bone. The two fused foot bones (third and fourth metapodials) found in the even-toed mammals such as deer, bison, and camels (artiodactyls).

Carnassial. Modified cheek tooth for cutting and tearing. Found in carnivores.

Carnivores. Meat-eating animals.

Cenozoic. The most recent era of the earth's past. Also called the Age of Mammals. Florida's accessible fossils date from this era. (65 million years ago to present.)

Cervical. Having to do with the neck.

Cervids. Deer and related animals.

Cetaceans. Whales, porpoises, and dolphins.

Crown. The grinding surface of a tooth.

Crustaceans. Crabs and barnacles.

Cretaceous Period. Preceded the Tertiary Period. During the Cretaceous, dinosaurs reached the height of their development. (136 to 65 million years before present.)

Distal. Furthest away from the body.

Dorsal. Referring to the back of an animal.

Echinoids. Sand dollars, sea stars, sea biscuits, and sea urchins. (Echinoderms.)

Edentates. Sloths, armadillos, and the extinct glyptodonts.

Eocene. An epoch of the Cenozoic Era extending from 54 to 37.5 million years before present.

Estuary. A river mouth where fresh and salt water environments meet.

Extant. Still living.

Extinct. No longer living.

Fauna. Animals.

Felids. Cat-like animals.

Flora. Plants.

Fluvatile. River gravel.

Foraminifera. Single-celled marine animals with calcium carbonate outer covering called tests. Important in the formation of some limestones.

Formation. A series of beds or strata that are essentially similar and were laid down over a definite period of time. Beds within the formation contain many identical fossils.

Gastropods. Shells with only one part, often coiled, such as conchs and snails. (univalves.)

Grazers. Herbivores that eat predominantly grass.

Herbivores. Plant-eating animals.

Hypsodont. High-crowned tooth.

In situ. Undisturbed or in place. Fossils found *in situ* are still in the same layer and position in which they were originally deposited.

Index fossil. A fossil that lived over a known and limited time. Such a fossil is a good indicator of the age of the bed in which it is found.

Invertebrates. Lower animals having no backbone. In this book, invertebrate refers to sea creatures such as mollusks, corals, barnacles, crabs, and sand dollars.

Karst. Limestone that has been partly dissolved by ground water to produce many holes — from tiny channels like a sponge to caves and underground rivers.

Mammals. Warm-blooded animals other than birds. Mammals have hair, give birth to live young, and nurse their young.

Mandible. Lower jaw.

Marine. Living in salt water.

Marl. Mixture of clay with shell or limestone.

Maxilla. Upper jaw.

Matrix. The material surrounding a fossil.

Miocene. An epoch of the Cenozoic Era extending from 24.5 to 5 million years before present.

Mollusks. Shells.

Neogene. Miocene to Recent; the last half of the Cenozoic Era.

Oligocene. An epoch of the Cenozoic Era extending from 37.5 to 24.5 million years before present.

Omnivores. Animals that eat a mixed diet.

Ostraderm. Bony plates found beneath the skin.

Paleocene. An epoch of the Cenozoic Era extending from 65 to 54 million years before present.

Paleogene. Paleocene through Oligocene; the first half of the Cenozoic Era.

Paleontology. The study of ancient life on earth.

Perissodactyls. The odd-toed hoofed mammals such as horse and rhinoceros.

Pleistocene. An epoch of the Cenozoic Era extending from 1.8 million to 10 thousand years before present.

Pliocene. An epoch of the Cenozoic Era extending from 5 to 1.8 million years before present.

Proboscidians. The elephant-like animals.

Proximal. Closest to the body.

Quaternary. The Cenozoic period which includes the Pleistocene and Recent epochs. (1.8 million years ago to present.)

Recent. The last epoch of the Cenozoic; the past 10 thousand years.

Reptiles. Cold-blooded animals such as alligators, snakes, and turtles.

Rodents. Rats, mice, squirrels, beavers, and related animals.

Ruminant. Herbivores having a three or more chambered stomach capable of breaking down cellulose. Ruminants include sheep, goats, cattle, deer, giraffes, bison, and antelope.

Screenwashing. A method of recovering fossils by washing them in a box having a bottom of window screen or hardware cloth.

Scute. Bony plate that forms the shell of turtles.

Terrestrial. Living on land.

Tertiary. The Cenozoic period up to the Pleistocene. (65 to 1.8 million years before present.)

Test. The limestone outer covering of echinoids and foraminifera.

Ungulates. Hoofed mammals.

Univalves. (gastropods) Shells with only one part, often coiled, such as conchs and snails.

Vertebra. Backbone.

Vertebrates. Animals with backbones — fish, amphibians, reptiles, birds, and mammals.

Vestigial. Remaining as a trace of something formerly present.

YBP. Years before present.

MORE INFORMATION ABOUT FOSSILS

The references listed below provide more information about fossils and particularly the wonderful ancient animals of Florida.

Florida Bureau of Geology Publications

A wealth of information about Florida is available in these inexpensive publications from the Florida Bureau of Geology. Those dealing with fossils are listed under the appropriate headings in this chapter, but other publications are available that describe Florida springs, sinkholes, rivers, and geologic formations. Many prove useful to the fossil hunter. Write to the Bureau of Geology for a complete list of publications:

Florida Bureau of Geology
903 W. Tennessee St.
Tallahassee, FL 32304

General Fossil Books

ARDUINI, PAOLO, 1986, Simon & Schuster's Guide to Fossils (Nature Guide Series): Simon & Schuster, New York.

CASANOVA, RICHARD and RONALD P. RATKEVICH, 1981, An Illustrated Guide to Fossil Collecting: Naturgraph Publishers, Inc., 240 pp.

COLBERT, E.H., 1980, A Fossil Hunter's Notebook (My Life With Dinosaurs and Other Friends): E. P. Dutton, New York.

FENTON, C. L. and M. A. FENTON, 1964, The Fossil Book: Doubleday and Co.

HAINES, TIM and P. CHAMBERS, 2006, The Complete Guide to Prehistoric Life: Firefly Books Ltd., United Kingdom.

KIRKALDY, J. F, 1984, Fossils in Color: Sterling Publishers, 224 pp.

MARTIN, PAUL, 2006, Twilight of the Mammoths: Ice Age Extinctions and the Rewilding of America: University of California Press.

MATTHEWS, WILLIAM H., 1962, Fossils, an Introduction into Prehistoric Life: Bames and Noble, Inc., 337 pp.

MOODY, RICHARD, Fossils - How to Find and Identify Over 300 Genera: Macmillan Publishing Co., 191 pp.

MOORE, LALICKER, and FISHER, 1952, Invertebrate Fossils: McGraw-Hill, 766 pp.

RANDAZZO, ANTHONY and DOUGLAS JONES, 1997, The Geology of Florida: University Press of Florida, Gainesville, FL.

THOMPSON, IDA, 1986, The Audubon Society Field Guide to North American Fossils: Alfred A. Knopf, Inc., 846 pp.

TURNER, ALAN, 2005, National Geographic Prehistoric Mammals: National Geographic Books.

WARD, CYRIL WALKER, 2002, Fossils (Smithsonian Handbooks): DK Publishing, Inc.

WARD, PETER D., 1997, The Call of Distant Mammoths: Sringer Verlag, New York.

Vertebrates

AUFFENBERG, W. A., 1958, Fossil turtles of the genus Terrapene in Florida: Bull. Fla. State Mus., vol. 3, no. 2, pp. 53–92.

AUFFENBERG, W. A., 1963, Fossil testudinine turtles of Florida: Tulane Stud. Zool., vol. 10, pp. 131–216.

AUFFENBERG, W. A., 1963, The fossil snakes of Florida: Tulane Stud. Zool., vol. 10, pp. 131–216.

BRODKORB, PIERCE, 1955, Avifauna of the Bone Valley Formation: Fla. Bureau of Geol. Report of Investigation No. 14, 59 pp.

BRODKORB, PIERCE, 1963. A Giant Flightless Bird from the Pleistocene of Florida: Auk, vol. 80, no. 2, pp. 111–115.

BRODKORB, PIERCE, 1963, Fossil birds from the Alachua Clays of Florida: Fla. Bureau of Geol. Spec. Pub. No. 2, Paper No. 4, pp. 1–17.

BASKIN, J., 1981, *Barbourofelis* (Nimravidae) and *Nimmvades* (Felidae), with a description of two new species from the late Miocene of Florida, Jour. Mamm., vol. 62, pp. 122–139.

CAMPBELL, K. E., JR., 1980, A review of the Rancholabrean avifauna of the Itchetucknee River, Florida: Contrib. Sci. Natur. Hist. Mus. Los Angeles County, vol. 330, pp. 119–129.

GARCIA, FRANK A., 1974, Illustrated Guide to Fossil Vertebrate: published by author, PO. Box 2131, Apollo Beach, FL 33570, 42 pp.

GUT, H. J., 1959, A Pleistocene vampire bat from Florida: J. Mamm. vol. 40, pp. 534–538.

GUT, H. J., and C. E. RAY, 1963, The Pleistocene vertebrate fauna of Reddick, Florida: Quar. J. Fla. Acad. Sci., vol. 26, pp. 315–328.

HAMON, J. HILL, 1964, The osteology and paleontology of the passerine birds of Reddick: Fla. Bureau of Geol. Bull. 44, 209 pp.

HIRSCHFELD, SUE, 1968, Vertebrate Fauna of Nichol's Hammock, a natural trap: Quart. J. Florida Acad. Sci., vol. 31, no. 3, pp. 177–189.

KELLOGG, R., 1944, Fossil cetaceans from the Florida Tertiary: Bull. Mus. of Comparative Zoology, Harvard University, vol. 94, no. 9, pp. 432–471.

KURTEN, BJORN, 1971, The Age of Mammals: Columbia University Press, 250 pp.

KURTEN, BJORN, 1980, Pleistocene Mammals of North America: Columbia University Press, 442 pp.

LEIDY, JOSEPH, 1889, Transactions of the Wagner Free Institute of Science of Philadelphia, Volume 2: Available from the Paleontological Research Institution, 1259 Trumansburg Road, Ithaca, NY 14850, 56pp.

MACFADDEN, BRUCE J., 1982, New species of primitive three-toed browsing horse from the Miocene phosphate mining district of Central Florida: Florida Scientist, vol. 45, pp. 117–126.

MACFADDEN, BRUCE J., 1984, Systematics and Phylogeny of *Hipparion, Neohipparion, Nannippus,* and *Cormohipparion* (Mammalia, Equidae) from the Miocene and Pliocene of the New World: Bull. Amer. Mus. Nat. Hist., vol. 179: Article 1, 189 pp.

MACFADDEN, BRUCE J., and JOHN S. WALDROP, 1980. *Nannippus phlegon* (Mammalia, Equidae) from the Pliocene (Blancan) of Florida: Bull. Florida State Mus., vol. 25, No. 1, pp. 1–37.

MACFADDEN, BRUCE J., and HENRY GAUANO, 1981. Late Hemphillian cat (Mammalia, Felidae) from the Bone Valley Formation of Central Florida: Jour. Paleonfc, vol. 55, no. 1, pp. 218–226.

MAGUO, V J., 1966, A revision of the fossil Selenodont Artiodactyls from the Middle Miocene Thomas Farm, Gilchrist County, Florida: Breviora, (Harvard University Mus. Comparative Zoology), vol. 255, pp. 1–27.

MEYLAN, E, 1982, The squammate reptiles of the Inglis IA Fauna: Bull. Fla. State Mus., vol. 27, pp. 1–85.

OLSEN, S. J., 1959, FossU mammals of Florida: Fla. Bureau of Geol. Special Publication No. 6, 74 pp.

PLASTER JACKET, issues one through 46, Vertebrate Paleontology, Florida State Museum.

RENZ, MARK, 2005, Giants in the Storm: Paleo Press, Lehigh Acres, FL.

ROBERTSON, J. S., 1976, Latest Pliocene mammals from Haile XV, Alachua County, Florida: Bull. Ha. State Mus., vol. 20, no. 3, pp. 111–186.

ROHMER, ALFRED S., 1966, Vertebrate Paleontology: University of Chicago Press, 468 pp.

ROHMER, ALFRED S., 1959, The Vertebrate Story: University of Chicago Press, 437 pp.

SCOTT, W B., 1962, A History of Land Mammals in the Western Hemisphere: Hafner Publishers, 800 pp.

STEHLI, FRANCIS G., and S. DAVID WEBB, 1985, The Great American Biotic Interchange: Plenum Publishing Co.

TEDFORD, R. H. and D. FRAILEY, 1976, Review of some carnivora (Mammalia) from the Thomas Farm local fauna (Hemingfordian: Gilchrist County, Florida): Am. Mus. Novitates, vol. 2610, pp. 1–9.

THOMAS, M. C., 1962, Fossil Vertebrates - Beach and Bank Collecting for Amateurs: c/o Florida Paleo. Society, Florida State Museum, Gainesville, FL 32611, 72 pp.

WEBB, S. DAVID, 1968, Underwater paleontology of Florida's rivers: National Geographic Society Research Reports, 1968 Projects, pp. 479–481.

WEBB, S. DAVID, 1969, The Pliocene canidae of Florida: Bull. Florida State Mus., vol. 14, no. 4, pp. 273–308.

WEBB, S. DAVID, 1973, Pliocene pronghorns of Florida: Jour. Mamm., vol. 54, no. 1, pp. 203–221.

WEBB, S. DAVID, 1974, Pleistocene Mammals of Florida: The University Presses of Florida, 259 pp.

WEBB, S. DAVID, 1982, The Great Inter-American Faunal Interchange: Science, vol. 215, pp. 1351–1357.

WEBB, S. DAVID, 1983, The rise and fall of the late Miocene ungulate fauna in North America: *in* Niteki, Matthew H., Coevolution, University of Chicago Press, pp. 267–306.

WEBB, S. DAVID, 1984, Ten Million Years of Mammal Extinctions in North America: *in* Martin, Paul S., and Richard G. Klein, Quaternary Extinctions — A Prehistoric Revolution: University of Arizona Press, pp. 189–209.

WEBB, S. DAVID and NORM TESSMAN, 1968. A Pliocene vertebrate fauna from low elevation in Manatee County, Florida: Am. Jour. Sci., vol. 266, pp. 777–810.

WEBB, S. DAVID, and B. J. MACFADDEN, and JON BASKIN, 1981, Geology and Paleontology of the Love Bone Bed from the Late Miocene of Florida: Amer. Jour. Sci., vol. 281, pp. 513–544.

WEBB, S. DAVID, JERALD T. MILANICH, ROGER ALEX-ON, and JAMES S. DUNBAR, 1984, A *Bison antiquus* kill site, Waeissa River, Jefferson County, Florida: American Antiquity, vol. 49, no. 2, pp. 389–392.

WEBB, S. DAVID and KENNETH WILKINS, 1984, Historical biogeography of Florida Pleistocene mammals: Special Publication Carnegie Museum of Natural History, no. 8, pp. 370–383.

WILKINS, K. E., 1984, Evolutionary trends in Florida Pleistocene pocket gophers (genus *Geomys*) with description of a new species: J. Vert. Paleont., vol. 3, pp. 166-181.

WOOD, H. E., 1964, Rhinoceroses from the Thomas Farm Miocene of Florida: Bull. Mus. Comp. Zool. Harvard, vol. 130, pp. 363–385.

Mixed Vertebrate and Invertebrate

Author not given. 2002, Fossil Species of Florida: A Publication of the Florida Paleontological Society, Inc. (Monographic series): Florida Paleontological Society, Gainesville, FL.

COMFORT, IRIS TRACY, 1998, Florida's Geological Treasures: Gem Guides Book Co., Baldwin Park, CA.

JEREMIAH, CLIFFORD J., 1980, Fiberglass Molding Techniques in Paleontology: Florida Paleontology Society, Inc., Florida State Museum, University of Florida, Gainesville, FL.

PETUCH, EDWARD J., Foreword by R. TUCKER ABBOTT, 1992, The Edge of the Fossil Sea: Life along the Shores of Prehistoric Florida: Bailey-Matthews Shell Museum, Sanibel Island, FL.

RUPERT, FRANK, 1994, A Fossil Hunter's Guide to the Geology of the Northern Florida Peninsula: Florida Geological Survey, Tallahassee, FL.

RUPERT, FRANK, 1994, A Fossil Hunter's Guide to the Geology of Panhandle Florida: Florida Geological Survey, Tallahassee, FL.

RUPERT, FRANK R., 1989, A Guide Map to Geologic and Paleontologic Sites in Florida: Florida Geological Survey, Tallahassee, FL.

SCOTT, T. M. and W. D. ALLMON (eds.), 1993, Plio-Pleistocene Stratigraphy and Paleontology of Southern Florida: Florida Geologic Survey Special Publication 36.

SCOTT, THOMAS M., and FRANK RUPERT, 1994, A Fossil Hunter's Guide to the Geology of Southern Florida: Florida Geological Survey, Tallahassee, FL.

SINIBALDI, ROBERT W., 1998, Fossil Diving in Florida's Waters: R.W. Sinibaldi, St. Petersburg, FL.

Mollusks

BRAYFIELD, W. and L., 1987, A Guide for Identifying Fossil Shells and Corals of Florida: 4140 Wood Duck Rd., Port Charlotte, FL 33953.

DUBAR, JULES R., 1958, Stratigraphy and paleontology of late Neogene strata of the Caloosahatchee River area of Southern Florida: Fla. Bureau of Geol. Bull. 40, 267 pp.

DUBAR, JULES R., 1962, Neogene biostratigraphy of the Charlotte Harbor area in Southwest Florida: Fla. Bureau of Geol. Bull. 43, 83 pp.

GARDNER, J. A., 1939, Notes on fossils from the Eocene of the Gulf Province II — the gastropod families Cassididae, Ficadae, and Buccinadae: U.S. Geol. Surv., Prof. Paper 193-B, pp. 18–44.

HARRIS, G. D., 1951, Preliminary note on Oeala bivalves: Bull. Am. Paleont., vol. 33, no. 138, pp. 1–54.

HEILPRIN, ANGELO, 1887, Explorations of the west coast of Florida and in the Okeechobee Wilderness: Wagner Free Inst. Sci. Phila. Trans., vol. 1, (1964 reprinted by Paleont. Research Inst., Ithaca, NY).

HOERLE, S. E., 1970, Mollusca of the "Glades" Unit of southern Florida, Part II — List of molluscan species from Belle Glade Rock Pit, Palm Beach Co., Florida: Tulane Stud. Geol. Paleont., vol. 8, no. 2, pp. 56–68.

HOERLE, S. E., 1976, The genus *Conus* (Mollusca: Gastropoda) from the Alum Bluff Group of north western Florida — and — A new species of *Conus* from the Chipola Formation: Tulane Stud. Geol. Paleont., vol. 12, no. 1., pp. 1–31.

MANSFIELD, W. C., 1924, Contributions to the late Tertiary and Quaternary paleontology of northwestern Florida: Fla. Geol. Surv., Ann. Rep. 15, pt. 2, pp. 25–51.

MANSFIELD, W. C., 1930, Miocene gastropods and scaphopods of the Choctowatehee Formation of Florida: Fla. Bureau of Geol. Bull. 3, 198 pp.

MANSFIELD, W. C., 1931, Some Tertiary mollusks from southern Florida: U.S. Nat'l. Mus. Proc., vol. 79, art. 21, pp. 1–12.

MANSFIELD, W. C., 1932, Miocene pelecypods of the Choctowatehee Formation of Florida: Fla. Bureau of Geol. Bull. 8, 240 pp.

MANSFIELD, W. C., 1932, Pliocene fossils from limestone in southern Florida: U.S. Geol. Surv., Prof. Paper 170-D, pp. 43–56.

MANSFIELD, W. C., 1935, New Miocene gastropods and scaphopods from Alaqua Creek Valley, Florida: Fla. Bureau of Geol. Bull. 12, 50 pp.

MANSFIELD, W. C., 1937, Mollusks of the Tampa and Suwannee limestones of Florida: Fla. Bureau of Geol. Bull. 15, 334 pp.

MANSFIELD, W. C., 1939, Notes on upper Tertiary and Pleistocene mollusks of peninsular Florida: Fla. Bureau of Geol. Bull. 18, 76 pp.

McGINITY, T. L., 1970, Mollusca of the "Glades" Unit of southern Florida, Part I - Introduction and observations: Tulane Stud. Geol. Paleont., vol. 8, no 2, pp. 51–56.

OLSON, A. A., 1967, Some Tertiary mollusks from south Florida and the Caribbean: Paleont. Research Inst, Ithaca, NY 62 pp.

OLSON, A. A., and ANNE HARRISON, 1953, Pliocene mollusks of southern Florida, etc.: Acad. Nat. Sci. Phila., Monograph 8, pp 1–457.

OLSON, A. A., and PETIT, R. E. 1964, Some Neogene mollusca from Florida and the Carolinas: Bull. Am. Paleont., vol. 47, no. 217, 71 pp.

PARKER, J. D., A new *Cassis,* and other mollusks from the
    Chipola Formation: Nautilus, vol. 61, no. 3, pp. 90–95.
RICHARDS, H. G., 1936, Fauna of the Pleistocene Pamlico
    Formation of the Southern Atlantic Coastal Plain:
    Geol. Soc. Am, Bull. vol. 76, no. 10, pp. 1611–1656.
RICHARDS, H. G., 1938, Marine Pleistocene of Florida: Geol.
    Soc. Am, Bull. 49, pp. 1267–1269.
RICHARDS, H. G., and K.V.W. PALMER, 1953, Eocene mol-
    lusks from Citrus and Levy counties, Florida: Fla.
    Bureau of Geol. Bull 35, 96 pp.
STANLEY, STEVEN M., 1986, Anatomy of regional mass
    extinction: Plio-Pleistocene decimation of the western
    Atlantic bivalve fauna: Palaios, vol. 1, pp. 17–36.
STUBBS, S. A., 1940, Pliocene mollusks from a well at
    Sanford, Florida: Jour. Paleont., vol. 14, no. 5, pp.
    510–514.
TUCKER, H. I., and DRUID WILSON, 1932, Some new and
    otherwise interesting fossils from the Florida Tertiary:
    Bull. Am. Jour. Paleont., vol. 18, no. 65, 15 pp.
TUCKER, H. I. and DRUID WILSON, 1933, A second contri-
    bution to the Neogene paleontology of south Florida:
    Bull. Am. Paleont., vol. 18, no. 66, 13 pp.
VOKES, H. E., 1969, Notes on the fauna of the Chipola
    Formation — a new species of *Eomiltha* (Molluska:
    Bivalvia): Tulane Stud. Geol. Paleont., vol. 7, no. 3,
    pp. 126–130.

Corals

VAUGHN, T. W., 1900, The Eocene and Oligocene corafaunas
    of the United States: U.S. Geol. Surv., Monograph 39.
WEISBORD, N. E., 1971, Corals from the Chipola and Jackson
    Bluff Formations of Florida: Fla. Bureau of Geol. Bull.
    53, 100 pp.
WEISBORD, N.E. 1973, New and little-known corals from the
    Tampa Formation of Florida: Fla. Bureau of Geol.
    Bull. 56, 156 pp.
WEISBORD, N.E. 1974, Late Cenozoic Corals of South
    Florida: Bull Am. Paleont, vol. 66, no. 285, pp.
    259–511.

Echinoids

COOKE C. WYTHE, 1959, Cenozoic Echinoids of the Eastern
    United States, U.S. Geol. Surv., Prof. Paper 321.
FISCHER, A. G., 1951, The Echinoid Fauna of the Inglis
    Member, Moody Branch Formation: Fla. Bureau of
    Geol. Bull. 34, pt. 2, 58 pp.
KIER, P. M., 1963, Tertiary echinoids from the Caloosahatchee
    and Tamiami Formations of Florida: Smithsonian
    Misc. Collections, vol. 145, no. 5, 63 pp.

Crustacea

RATHBUN, M. J., 1935, Fossil Crustacea of the Atlantic and
    Gulf Coastal Plains: Geol. Soc. Am, Special Paper #2.
WILLIAMS, A. B., 1984, Shrimps, Lobsters and Crabs of the
    Atlantic Coast: Smithsonian Institution Press, 550 pp.

Appendix A
Florida Fossil Permit

FLORIDA STATUTE § 1004.57 sets forth the State of Florida's declared intent to protect and preserve vertebrate fossils and vertebrate paleontology sites. All vertebrate fossils found on lands owned or leased by the state belong to the state with title to the fossils vested in the Florida Museum of Natural History for the purposes of administration. Field collection of vertebrate fossils may be conducted under the authority of a permit issued by the Program of Vertebrate Paleontology in accordance with FS § 1004.575 and the University of Florida RULE 6C1-7.541 F.A.C. The purpose of the fossil collecting permit is not only to manage this non-renewable part of Florida's heritage, but to help paleontologists learn more about the range and distribution of the state's fossil animals.

WHAT AREAS ARE COVERED? The state intends to encourage preservation of its heritage wherever vertebrate fossils are discovered; the state encourages all persons having knowledge of such fossils to notify the Program of Vertebrate Paleontology at the Florida Museum of Natural History. A permit is required for most collecting activities on all lands owned or leased by the state. This includes sites located either on submerged lands or uplands. Please note that existing regulations prohibit collecting in state parks and certain other managed areas. Check the regulations to see if your activities are covered. Fossil collecting on private land does not require a permit (but you will need the permission of the land owner or manager to enter, collect on, and retain fossils from private property). Having a permit does not give you the right to collect fossils on private property without the permission of the land owner.

WHAT OBJECTS ARE COVERED? It is Florida's public policy to protect and preserve vertebrate fossils, including bones, teeth, natural casts, molds, impressions, and other remains of prehistoric vertebrate animals. Fossil sharks teeth are specifically excluded from these regulations, as are the fossils of plants, invertebrate animals (e.g., mollusks, sea urchins, crabs, etc.), and other organisms, so no permit is required to collect such specimens. A permit is required to collect fossils of all other kinds of vertebrates, namely fish (except shark teeth), amphibians, reptiles, birds, and mammals.

WHO MAY OBTAIN A PERMIT? Any person with an interest in Florida vertebrate fossils may apply for a permit. These regulations apply to both residents and non-residents of Florida. Minors can apply for permits, but may also collect with a permit-carrying adult parent or guardian who assumes all responsibilities and obligations for the collected specimens.

WHO MUST OBTAIN A PERMIT? Any person or entity buying, selling or trading vertebrate fossils found on or under state-owned or leased land; and/or

Any person or entity engaged in the systematic collection, acquisition, or restoration of vertebrate fossils found on state-owned or leased land.

"Systematic collection" is hereby characterized by one or more of the following three features:

volume of collections of vertebrate fossils in excess of one gallon at one site;

use of any power-driven machinery or mechanical excavating tools of any size or hand tools greater than two (2) feet in length;

the collection, acquisition, excavation, salvage, exhumation or restoration of vertebrate fossils at a site on more than three days or a maximum of twenty-four hours during a period of one year.

HOW IS A PERMIT OBTAINED? Any person wishing to engage in field collection of vertebrate fossils on land owned or leased by the state of Florida should apply for a permit by printing out and completing an application form and mailing it to

Florida Program of Vertebrate Paleontology
Florida Museum of Natural History
University of Florida
Gainesville, Florida 32611-7800

The application must be accompanied by a self-identification document such as a photocopy of the applicant's birth certificate, driver's license, or passport, and a check or money order for $5.00 US made payable to the Florida Program of Vertebrate Paleontology. A permit shall be issued for one year. A multiple-user permit will be granted to an individual representing an organization or institution. Multiple-user permits are not intended for collective use by separate adult members of a family or household; they should each apply for their own permits.

WHAT OBLIGATIONS DOES A PERMIT CARRY? As a permit holder you can help unlock the secrets of Florida's fossil heritage and preserve this knowledge for future generations. Each year permittees add new discoveries to Florida's fossil heritage. The holder of a permit must report any unusual specimen or unusually rich site to the Florida Program of Vertebrate Paleontology as soon as possible. At any convenient time, no later than the end of the permit year, the permit holder shall submit to the Florida Program of Vertebrate Paleontology a list of all vertebrate fossils collected during the permit year along with appropriate locality information; or the actual collections with appropriate locality information. If within sixty (60) days of receipt of the list or the actual collection the Florida Program of Vertebrate Paleontology does not request the permittee to donate one or more of the fossils collected, they may be released as "non-essential fossils" to be disposed of however the permit holder may choose.

If you already have a fossil permit, you should renew it about three to four weeks before the expiration date to ensure that you receive your new card before the old one expires. Unless you indicate otherwise, the starting date for the renewed permit will be one day after your current permit expires.

Questions about Florida Program of Vertebrate Paleontology may be directed to:

Richard Hulbert
Program of Vertebrate Paleontology
Florida Museum of Natural History
University of Florida
Gainesville, Florida 32611
Tel: (352)392-1721 Ext. 259
E-mail: rhulbert@flmnh.ufl.edu

Florida Fossil Permit Application

This application is for a permit that will entitle the person named on the permit to collect, for the period of one (1) year, vertebrate fossils on land owned or leased by the State of Florida. The permittee must abide by all the provisions contained in Florida Statutes § 1004.575-576 and the University of Florida Regulation implementing this law.

Persons who already have a permit and wish to renew it for an additional year should not use this form. They should follow the instructions found online at http://www.flmnh.ufl.edu/vertpaleo/renewpermit.htm instead.

Print out and mail completed application to:

Program of Vertebrate Paleontology
Florida Museum of Natural History
University of Florida
Gainesville, Florida 32611-7800

The following must be enclosed with the filled-out application:

Photocopy of applicant's identification document (i.e., driver's license, birth certificate, or passport).

Check or money order for $5.00 in U.S. currency payable to the Program of Vertebrate Paleontology. If you are sending two or more applications, just send one check for the total amount, not multiple checks of $5. **PLEASE DO NOT SEND CASH.**

Applicant's Full Name (must match that on identification document):

_____

Complete Mailing Address (include zip code):

_____

_____

Telephone (include area code):

_____

E-mail address (optional):

_____

I, the undersigned, affirm that I will abide by Florida Statutes § 1004.575-576 and the Regulations of the Program of Vertebrate Paleontology, University of Florida Rule 6C1-7.541 F.A.C.

Signature: _____

Date: _____

Appendix B

Fossil Collections and Displays in the State

Many regional natural history museums, youth museums, university museums and nature centers have fossil displays. Often staff members can help with fossil identification and suggestions of good places to hunt. Some of these are listed below:

1. Bailey-Matthews Shell Museum
3075 Sanibel-Captiva Road
Sanibel, FL 33957
Has an outstanding exhibit of Florida fossil shells.

2. The Southwest Florida Museum of Natural History
2300 Peck Street
Fort Myers, FL 33901
Features an exhibit on Paleo-Florida with a display of Florida Ice Age fossils.

3. Museum of Arts and Sciences
1040 Museum Boulevard
Daytona Beach, FL 32014
Has a beautifully restored skeleton of the giant ground sloth Eremotherium and other Pleistocene vertebrates from the Daytona Bone Bed.

4. The Florida Museum of Natural History
P.O. Box 117800
Gainesville, FL 32611-7800
Contains several displays of Florida fossil animals plus a diorama depicting paleontologists recovering Bone Valley fossils from a phosphate mine.

5. South Florida Science Museum
4801 Dreher Trail North
West Palm Beach, FL 33405
Has some Florida Pleistocene fossils, mostly vertebrates.

6. South Florida Museum
201 10th Street West
Bradenton, FL 33505
Contains vertebrate fossils including bison, camel, horse, manatee, and whale.

7. The Conservancy Nature Center
1450 Merrihue Drive
Naples, FL 33942
Features representative vertebrate remains, three dioramas of prehistoric Florida, and fossil shells of Miocene-Pliocene age.

8. The Old Cutler Hammock Nature Center
17555 SW 79th Avenue
Miami, FL 33157
Displays the vertebrate and invertebrate fossil finds excavated from a sinkhole found in Old Cutler Hammock. This abundant late Pleistocene fauna is displayed at the nearby
Charles Deering Estate
16701 SW 72nd Avenue
Miami, FL 33157

Appendix C

Fossils on the Web

Paleontological Resources for Fossil Collectors at http://www.flmnh.ufl.edu/natsci/vertpaleo/resources/res.htm, This Florida Natural History Museum site is excellent for all persons interested in fossils and fossil collecting. It provides information on every aspect of paleontology from field collection techniques, to preparation and mounting of the fossils, to casting and moldmaking. Here, you can also find helpful references to books and professional papers dealing with paleontology, as well as addresses of vendors who sell supplies, equipment, and chemicals used in collecting and preparing fossils. You can find out what fossil clubs are located in your area and how you can acquire a fossil-collecting permit to collect on state lands and rivers in Florida.

The Fossil Horse Cybermuseum site, offered by the Florida Natural History Museum at http://www.flmnh.ufl.edu/natsci/vertpaleo/fhc/firstCM.htm, provides an excellent introduction to hoofed mammal fossils in Florida.

The Florida Electronic Library at http://www.flelibrary.org/ offers select internet access to comprehensive, active, and reliable information. Available resources include electronic magazines, newspapers, magazines, and books. Florida fossil coverage is excellent; many state publications difficult to find elsewhere are listed. The only requirement for use is any Florida public library card — simply enter the numbers below the barcode.

The websites of Florida Public libraries are listed at www.publiclibraries.com/florida.htm. They enable the searcher to find the books, periodicals, and technical publications dealing with fossils in Florida that are carried by each library. Many give brief descriptions of the publication and the library branch where the material is available.

The State Library of Florida at dlis.dos.state.fl.us/Library/ offers books on fossils and access to state publications useful to fossil hunters. Some material can be read only in the library.

Universities of the State of Florida list their library facilities and many are available for general (non-student) use. A good example is the University of South Florida library site http://www.lib.usf.edu/.

Fossil Expeditions Newsletter at http://www.fossilexpeditions.com/news.htm is a quality site produced by author and expert fossil finder Mark Renz who heads **Wild Tours** (http://www.fossilexpeditions.com), offering Florida fossil expeditions. The newsletter offers practical advice on techniques and locations for fossil hunters.

Appendix D

Time Span of Florida Mammals of the Past Ten Million Years

	Miocene	Pliocene	Pleistocene	Recent
Million years	10........9........8........7........6........5	........4........3........2.	.......1.......	0

Name

Didelphis
(opossum)

Holmesina
(giant armadillo)

Dasypus bellus
(armadillo)

Eremotherium
(giant ground sloth)

Glossotherium
(ground sloth)

Casteroides
(giant beaver)

Castor
(beaver)

Peromyscus
(cotton mouse)

Sigmadon
(hispid cotton rat)

Neochoerus
(giant capybara)

Hydrochoerus
(capybara)

Osteoborus
(hyenoid dog)

Borophagus
(hyenoid dog)

Arctodus
(short-faced bear)

Tremarctos
(short-faced bear)

Procyon
(raccoon)

Mephitis
(skunk)

Barbouro-felis

Nimravides

Smilodon
(saber-cat)

204

	Miocene				Pliocene			Pleistocene	Recent

Million years 10........9.......8.......7.......6.......5........4.......3.....2.......1.......0

Name

Pliomastodon

Mammut
(mastodons)

Gomphotherium

Amebelodon
(shovel-tusked
gomphothere)

Rhynchotherium

Cuvieronius

Mammuthus
(mammoth)

Tapirus
(tapir)

Aphelops
(rhinoceros)

Teleoceras
(rhinoceros)

Merrychippus
(three-toed horse)

Nannipus
(three-toed horse)

Astrohippus

Dinohippus

Equus

Platygonus
(peccary)

Mylohyus
(peccary)

Kyptoceras
(bent-horned
protoceratid)

Hemiauchenia
(camelid)

Paleolama
(camelid)

Odocoileus
(deer)

Hexameryx
(six-horned
antilocaprid)

Antilocapra
(antelope)

Bison

Adapted from S. David Webb, "Ten Million Years of Mammal Extinctions," in Martin and Klein, *Quaternary Extinctions — A Prehistoric Revolution.*

Appendix E
Fossil Clubs in Florida

**Imperial Bone Valley Gem, Mineral, and Fossil Society —
Polk County**
> P.O. Box 2054, Auburndale, FL 33823.
> Website: http://www.bonevalley.net
> Meets monthly at the Bartow Civic Center.

Florida Fossil Hunters — Orlando
> P.O. Box 540404, Orlando, FL 32854–0404.
> Website: http://www.floridafossilhunters.com
> E-mail: info@floridafossilhunters.com
> Meets monthly at the Orlando Science Center.

Florida Paleontological Society, Inc. — Gainesville
> Florida Museum of Natural History, University of
> Florida, Gainesville, FL 32611.
> E-mail: fps@flmnh.ufl.edu
> Meets twice a year — spring and fall. Functions as a
> liaison between Florida Museum of Natural History
> and amateurs statewide.

Fossil Club of Lee County — Fort Myers
> Website: http://www.fcolc.com
> Meets monthly at the Calusa Nature Center, 3450 Ortiz
> Avenue, Fort Myers.

Fossil Club of Miami — Miami
> Website: http://www.geocities.com/
> miamifossilclub/index.html
> E-mail: MiamiFossilWeb@aol.com
> Meets monthly at the Miami Museum of Science, 3280
> South Miami Ave.

Manasota Fossil Club — Sarasota
> P.O. Box 1601, Tallevast, FL 34270
> Website: http://mywebpages.comcast.net/ccopas/
> manasota.htm
> E-mail: ccopas@comcast.net
> Meets monthly at the Sarasota County
> Library east of I-75 off Fruitville Road.

Sanibel-Captiva Shell Club — Sanibel Island
> Website: www.sanibelcaptivashellclub.com
> Meets the last Sunday of the month at 2 p.m.,
> April–October, at the Bailey Matthew Shell Museum.

Southwest Florida Fossil Club — Punta Gorda
> Website: http://www.southwestfloridafossilclub.com
> E-mail: info@southwestfloridafossilclub.com
> Meets monthly at Edison Community College.

Tampa Bay Fossil Club — Tampa
> P.O. Box 673, Palm Harbor, FL 34682
> Web Site: www.tampabayfossilclub.com
> E-mail: tampabayfossilclub@juno.com
> Meets monthly at University of South Florida.

Index

Boldface indicates pages on which illustrations appear, even if the subject of the illustration is dealt with in the text on those same pages.